AF271587

WSI | Mitteilungen

Hans **Böckler**
Stiftung ▬▬

Zeitschrift des Wirtschafts- und Sozialwissenschaftlichen Instituts
der Hans-Böckler-Stiftung

» Special Issue 2019

Martin Behrens
Heiner Dribbusch [eds.]

Industrial
Relations
in Germany

Dynamics and Perspectives

The Deutsche Nationalbibliothek lists this publication in the
Deutsche Nationalbibliografie; detailed bibliographic data
are available on the Internet at http://dnb.d-nb.de

ISBN   978-3-8487-5974-3 (Print)
        978-3-7489-0057-3 (ePDF)

British Library Cataloguing-in-Publication Data
A catalogue record for this book is available from the British Library.

ISBN   978-3-8487-5974-3 (Print)
        978-3-7489-0057-3 (ePDF)

Library of Congress Cataloging-in-Publication Data
Behrens, Martin / Dribbusch, Heiner
Industrial Relations in Germany
Dynamics and Perspectives
Martin Behrens / Heiner Dribbusch (eds.)
150 pp.
Includes bibliographic references.

ISBN   978-3-8487-5974-3 (Print)
        978-3-7489-0057-3 (ePDF)

ISSN   0342-300X

1st Edition 2019
© Nomos Verlagsgesellschaft/edition sigma, Baden-Baden, Germany 2019. Printed
and bound in Germany.
This work is subject to copyright. All rights reserved. No part of this publication may
be reproduced or transmitted in any form or by any means, electronic or mechanical,
including photocopying, recording, or any information storage or retrieval system,
without prior permission in writing from the publishers. Under § 54 of the German
Copyright Law where copies are made for other than private use a fee is payable to
"Verwertungsgesellschaft Wort", Munich.
No responsibility for loss caused to any individual or organization acting on or refraining
from action as a result of the material in this publication can be accepted by Nomos
or the editors.

Table of Contents

Industrial Relations in Germany – Dynamics and Perspectives
Introduction

MARTIN BEHRENS, HEINER DRIBBUSCH, ANKE HASSEL

The Institute of Economic and Social Research (WSI) is trade-union related academic research institute. Since its foundation in 1946, the focus of the WSI has been on the improvement of life chances, social justice and fair working and living conditions. In 1995 it became part of the Hans-Böckler-Stiftung, a non-profit foundation of the German Confederation of Trade Unions (DGB), fostering co-determination, promoting research and supporting students. Based on sound academic analysis, the researchers of the WSI elaborate policy proposals aimed at overcoming labour market restrictions and social problems to the benefit of employees. The main fields of research of the WSI are social and labour market policy, gender studies with a focus on job inequalities and industrial and labour relations. The WSI Collective Agreement Archive is the major German information centre on developments of collectively-agreed pay and conditions. Research on Germany is complemented by active participation of scholars in international networks investigating social and labour market policies, working conditions and industrial relations at the European and global level.

With this special English edition of its academic journal *WSI-Mitteilungen,* the WSI revisits a theme it had previously explored in a special issue on the occasion of the 2003 IIRA World Congress in Berlin. Under the title *Industrial Relations in Germany – an Empirical Survey,* the 2003 issue focused on the state of works councils and multi-employer collective bargaining; the core institutional pillars which have shaped the dual system of German industrial relations. Back in 2003 the WSI was concerned with the simultaneous decline of membership in both employers' associations and trade unions and the risks of a slow but steady erosion of collective bargaining. The institute nevertheless remained confident about the stability and flexibility of the German system of labour relations although it stressed the necessity for stabilisation measures to be taken by the bargaining parties and the government.

In 2019 it is apparent that since 2003 labour relations in Germany have undergone a turbulent history. It is the aim of this special issue to contribute towards improving our understanding of changes in German labour relations but also to identify new perspectives in both the theory and practice of industrial relations. The erosion of the bargaining system certainly did not stop as bargaining coverage retreated even further; despite considerable efforts to strengthen consolidation, overall union membership continued to decline and the share of members in employers' associations which remained committed to multi-employer bargaining continued to shrink. But just when it appeared that the "pillars of social partnership" were doomed to crumble the Great Recession of 2008 arrived and changed the game. Unions, employers, works councils and the state joined forces in a "crisis version" of German corporatism. Supported by a favourable economic development the resulting "German job miracle" was considered to be proof of the virtues of the German model in general and a renaissance of the unions in particular.

The Great Recession was followed by the so-called European public debt crisis. The European Union, supported by the German government, responded to this with a set of policy changes that have come to be known as the "new European economic governance". Part of this governance was a shift within the EU in favour of political intervention in national bargaining outcomes and procedures. But while the so-called "crisis countries" were forced to dismantle collective social security and decentralise their collective bargaining systems, Germany took another direction. In response to a campaign by the unions, which was met with broad public support, a statutory national minimum wage was introduced with effect from 1 January 2015. Much of the formal stability of German industrial relations is owed to the fact that no major political party questions its foundations. The decline of bargaining coverage and the shrinking of the presence of works councils is a matter of concern for both Christian and Social Democrats. The existence of strong unions is not put into question, not least because they are considered to be more a factor of social stability than of public disorder. Against the background of a long economic upswing since 2010, Germany has seen a substantial increase in employment and unions have not only been able to secure an increase in real wages but also achieve new models of working time which reflect the changing needs of employees.

However, despite all public and political acclaim, the erosion of the German model has continued. The picture of German industrial relations has become more uneven and the differentiation between labour relations and working conditions has widened. In 2019 bargaining coverage is at its lowest level in post-war German history. Although multi-sector bargaining is still the norm, a majority of employees no longer work under a collective agreement. The decline is particularly pronounced in private services. In major sectors such as the retail industry, collective bargaining covers barely a third of employees. Opening clauses allowing for (temporary) deviations from collectively agreed provisions are in 2019 no longer an exception but the norm. Although the national minimum wage stabilised the wage floor, it has not prevented Germany retaining one of the largest low-wage sectors in Europe. The 2003 call for stabilising measures from below and from above is therefore in 2019 as relevant as it was then (see the contribution by *Thorsten Schulten* in this volume).

The picture is similar if we look at the scope of workplace representation and co-determination. The situation at major car manufacturers such as Mercedes or Volkswagen, where strong works councils supported by a well-organised workforce appear to be on a level playing field with management, is not typical for the vast majority of establishments. In 2019 a majority of employees in the private sector work in establishments without a works council and works councils are largely absent in small and medium-sized workplaces. Again, it is in private services where the situation is particularly bleak; while it is questionable whether all employees, particularly in very small workplaces, deem a works council necessary to defend their interests, there are recent findings which underpin past observations that some employers are not only hostile towards works councils but actively obstruct employees' efforts to establish one (see *Behrens/Dribbusch*). Since 1997 the WSI has regularly surveyed existing works councils to learn more about their approaches and attitudes and also about their composition. A significant fact revealed in recent analysis shows that women and part-time employees tend to be under-represented in works councils (see *Emmler/Brehmer*). It comes perhaps as no surprise that across industries members of a works council are more likely to be union members than the employees they represent.

As both bargaining coverage and the existence of a works council are closely linked to union presence and union activity, the decline of union density in Germany is a decisive factor for the balance of power which shapes industrial relations at industry and plant level. As a closer look at the state of German employment relations reveals, we find diverse patterns within different sectors of the German economy. While unions have regained stability or even increased their presence in some organising territories, they have faced continuous decline in others. Focusing on collective bargaining and works council coverage, *Hassel/Schroeder* distinguish three different patterns or "worlds" of labour relations. In contrast to what we see in other European countries, it is less the shrinking public sector but the large companies in manufacturing that constitute the "first world". It is here where industrial relations come closest to the ideal type of the German model. However, this world is not detached from a "third world" of deregulation which appears much less prominently in international comparative research than the world of social partnership with which German industrial relations have been frequently identified.

Industrial relations do not come without conflict and Germany is no exception to this. A comparatively recent development in Germany is the tertiarisation of conflict; with the migration of militancy from manufacturing to services (see *Dribbusch*). This development is closely linked to the removal of collective security as a result of privatising the public sector and a fiscal policy which has impoverished public budgets. Added to this comes an awareness on the side of unions that the times are over when the commitment of employers to collective bargaining and regular pay increases could be taken for granted.

In 2003 the WSI remained tacitly optimistic that some core features of the German model of co-determination could positively help to develop a forthcoming European model of labour relations in a non neo-liberal direction. In 2019 we have to acknowledge that this did not happen. It was rather the German model of industrial relations which was shaped by the EU in the form of the Court of Justice of the European Union (CJEU). A number of decisions by the court intervened in the power relationship between employers and employees (see *Seikel/Absenger*). By restricting the scope, applicability, and the contents of collective agreements the CJEU *de facto* furthered the erosion of the German model.

For a long time, German labour relations have been conceptualised by referring to a rather homogeneous model. While different names have been used to describe this model such as "the dual system of interest representation", "social partnership" or "the German model", they were all based on the assumption that they capture the very essence of what regulates labour relations in a variety of different workplaces. As the authors of this volume indicate, such a perspective becomes increasingly outdated as the diversity of different institutions and practices increases. Directions of change seem to follow different and sometimes even contradictory paths. As is outlined in this volume, we find processes such as decentralisation and Europeanisation of labour relations side by side with the (partial) growth of state involvement, as well as the weakening of collective actors such as unions and employers' associations. We hope that the analyses in this volume, some of them available in English for the first time, contribute to a better understanding of the forces at work in the process of changing German labour relations.

AUTHORS

MARTIN BEHRENS, PD Dr., is Senior Researcher at the Institute of Economic and Social Research (WSI) within the Hans-Böckler-Foundation in Düsseldorf, Germany. His field of research covers labour relations in national and comparative perspectives, including employers' associations, works councils and trade unions.

@ E-Mail: Martin-Behrens@boeckler.de

HEINER DRIBBUSCH, Dr. rer. pol., is Senior Researcher at the Institute of Economic and Social Research (WSI) within the Hans-Böckler-Foundation in Düsseldorf, Germany. His field of research covers industrial relations with a special focus on trade unionism, collective bargaining and industrial conflicts.

@ E-Mail: Heiner-Dribbusch@boeckler.de

ANKE HASSEL, Prof. Dr., from 2016 until 2019 Scientific Director of the Institute of Economics and Social Sciences (WSI) of the Hans-Böckler-Foundation. Main areas of work: industrial relations, labour market, social policy.

@ E-Mail: Hassel@hertie-school.org

German Collective Bargaining – from Erosion to Revitalisation?

Following a continuous decrease in levels of collective bargaining coverage for more than two decades, all relevant social actors in Germany now agree that something has to be done to reverse that trend. However, there are still rather different views among trade unions, employers' associations and political actors about the right measures and instruments required for a revitalisation of collective bargaining. While the unions try to rebuild their organisational power and gain political support for the bargaining system, the employers demand further flexibilisation in order to make agreements more attractive for the companies.

THORSTEN SCHULTEN

1 Introduction

German collective bargaining, as it evolved during the 1950s in the post-war period, was for a long time rightly regarded as a prototype of an "inclusive collective bargaining system" (Hayter 2015). A comprehensive structure of sector-level multi-employer bargaining ensured a high bargaining coverage whereby between 80 and 90 per cent of all workers in Germany were covered by collective agreements. Since the mid-1990s, however, a continuous decrease in bargaining coverage has led to a significant level of erosion.

Against that background, the academic discourse on German industrial relations and collective bargaining was long dominated by the view that the erosion is an almost inevitable development (e. g. Hassel 1999; Hassel/Schulten 1998, Streeck 2009). In the recent decade, however, the discourse has largely changed from a "paradigm of crisis to a paradigm of strategy" (Urban 2013), putting much more emphasis on the strategic options of social actors to shape the developments of industrial relations. The change in the discourse came largely from the trade union literature and its new emphasis on organising practices (Brinkmann et al. 2008), but was also adopted in the debates on the future of German collective bargaining (Bispinck et al. 2010).

In the meantime, the question on how to revitalise collective bargaining has become one of the core issues in German industrial relations. The changing views and perspectives have largely been influenced by the role industrial relations played in overcoming the great economic recession in 2009 (Lesch et al. 2017a). Moreover, the comparatively good economic performance and the sharp decrease in unemployment during the 2010s have significantly re-strengthened the structural power of German trade unions (Dribbusch et al. 2018). Finally, there was also the consideration of international experiences, which supported the view that the erosion of German collective bargaining was not an irreversible process but could be politically shaped and influenced (Bispinck et al. 2010).

Since the 2010s, the idea that Germany needs a fundamental revitalisation of collective bargaining has become more and more an issue not only for the trade unions but also for sections of the employers and even for most political parties; including the current government coalition of Christian and Social Democrats. One expression for the changing discourse was the adoption of the Law for the Strengthening of Collective Bargaining Autonomy *(Gesetz zur Stärkung der Tarifautonomie)* in 2014 which included a legal package of different new regulations including the introduction of a statutory minimum wage and a facilitation of the rules for the extension of collective agreements.

This article is basically composed of two parts. The first part contains a detailed analysis of the development of collective bargaining in Germany and elaborates the available data on collective bargaining coverage (section 2). In the second part, the fundamental approaches and concrete proposals for a revitalisation of German collective bargaining are discussed (section 3). Finally, it concludes with a short outlook on the future of collective bargaining in Germany (section 4).

2 Decline in Collective Bargaining Coverage

2.1 Different Data Sources for Measuring Bargaining Coverage

Although all collective agreements in Germany have to be registered at the Federal Ministry of Labour there is no administrative data available on the number of workers covered by collective agreements. All data on collective bargaining coverage in Germany is based on company and worker surveys. There are three major data sources available:

The first and most widely used data source is the IAB Establishment Survey carried out by the Institute for Employment Research *(Institut für Arbeitsmarkt- und Berufsforschung, IAB)* of the German Federal Employment Agency which is an annual survey of more than 15 000 establishments. Based on that survey the IAB regularly publishes elaborations on collective bargaining coverage in Germany (for the most recent reports: Ellguth/Kohaut 2018, 2019; Kohaut 2018). The second data source is the German Socio-Economic Panel (SOEP) which is an annual survey of around 30 000 individuals in approximately 11 000 private households. As only the most recent waves of the SOEP provide some information on whether or not the surveyed workers are hired in companies with collective agreements, there is currently only one study available which analyses the collective bargaining coverage on the basis of the SOEP data (Schneider/Vogel 2018). Finally, the third data source is the German Structure of Earnings Survey (SES) which is by far the largest of the three surveys with around 60 000 surveyed establishments. The SES is carried out only every four years so that currently the latest available data is from 2014. The German Federal Statistical Office has produced comprehensive data evaluation on collective bargaining coverage in Germany based on the 2014 SES data (Statistisches Bundesamt 2016).

Although all three surveys provide a representative profile of the German

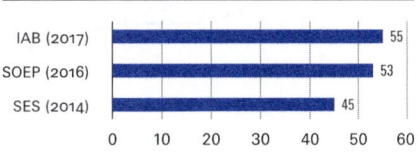

FIGURE 1

Collective bargaining coverage in Germany according to different data sources

Percentage shares of workers employed in companies covered by collective agreements

IAB (2017)	55
SOEP (2016)	53
SES (2014)	45

Sources: IAB = Establishment Panel of the Institute for Employment Research 2017 (Ellguth/Kohaut 2018); SOEP = German Socio-Economic Panel 2016 (Schneider/Vogel 2018); SES = German Structure of Earnings Survey 2014 (Statistisches Bundesamt 2016)

WSI Mitteilungen

economy regarding company sizes, branches and regions, they come to significantly different conclusions regarding collective bargaining coverage in Germany *(figure 1)*. According to the IAB Establishment Survey in 2017, around 55 per cent of all German workers were employed in a company covered by a collective agreement. According to the SOEP in 2016, the figure was only 53 per cent, while the SES in 2014 found even a much lower figure of only 45 per cent.

This article will take the figures provided by the IAB Establishment Survey as this is the only data source which allows the creation of more long-term data series. Considering the different results of all three surveys, however, it might be concluded that even the IAB Establishment Survey underestimates the real decline in bargaining coverage in Germany.

2.2 Development of Bargaining Coverage Since the Mid-1990s

According to the data from the IAB Establishment Panel, Germany has been faced by a strong and continuous decline in bargaining coverage (Oberfichtner/Schnabel 2017, Ellguth/Kohaut 2018, 2019; Kohaut 2018). The percentage of workers employed in companies with collective agreements declined from almost 80 per cent in the mid-1990s to a mere 55 per cent in 2017 *(figure 2)*. The decline was particularly strong in the second half of the 1990s but continued during the 2000s and 2010s.

The reasons for that decline were manifold: It started after German unification which promoted a more fundamental transformation of German capitalism and the political economy (Lehndorff et al. 2009; Streeck 2009). At the same time, neoliberal percep-

FIGURE 2

Collective bargaining coverage in Germany

Percentage shares of workers employed in companies covered by collective agreements

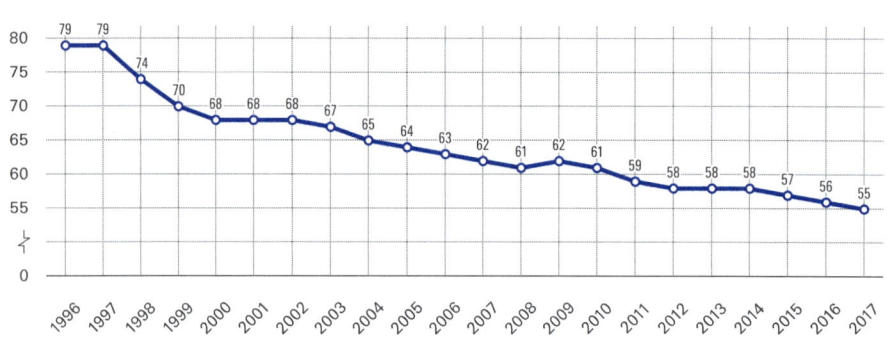

Source: IAB Establishment Panel

tions of globalisation became a dominant discourse in Germany which put all social and labour-market institutions under the general suspicion of hampering international competitiveness (Flecker/Schulten 1999). Against that background collective bargaining lost a lot of acceptance among German employers who complained about labour costs being "too high" as a result of "overregulated" and "non-flexible" collective agreements (Hassel/Schulten 1998). Thus, the employers demanded a more fundamental decentralisation of German collective bargaining. Since the mid-2000s, there is almost no sectoral collective bargaining area where the bargaining parties have not agreed on more or less far-reaching opening-clauses with the opportunity to diverge from sectoral standards at company level (Schulten/Bispinck 2018). However, this far-reaching decentralisation has not been able to stop the decline in bargaining coverage. On the contrary, Germany has seen a parallel development of organised and disorganised decentralisation or even erosion of collective bargaining.

The decreasing acceptance of collective agreements has been particularly strong among newly-established firms. The decline of bargaining coverage has therefore not only been the result of employers withdrawing from collective agreements but even more of a "composition effect" as new firms have been less willing to participate in collective bargaining (Ellguth/Kohaut 2010; Bossler 2019). The development has also directly impacted German employers' associations who have been afraid that the lower acceptance of collective agreements might be transformed into a lower number of organised employers. In order to avoid membership losses many German employers' associations have introduced a new so-called "OT" membership status (OT = *ohne*

Tarifbindung, which means "not bound by collective agreement") according to which organised employers can *de facto* choose whether or not they want to be bound by the sectoral agreements signed by the association (Behrens/Helfen 2019).

According to survey data provided by Behrens/Helfen (2016, p. 453), in the meantime about half of all German employers have introduced the possibility of a so-called "OT" membership status. To what extent employers make use of this "OT" membership in practice is rather unclear, as most employers' associations do not publish any data on their membership. One of the few exceptions is the metal industry where according to the employers' association *Gesamtmetall,* the percentage of companies using an "OT" membership status increased from around 25 per cent in 2006 to about 52 per cent in 2017 *(figure 3).* As larger companies are more likely to be covered by a collective agreement, the percentage of workers in an organised company with an "OT" status is around 22 per cent. All in all, the figures show an ongoing shift in the membership towards "OT" members. There is again a particular role of newly-established firms. If they become a member of an employers' association at all, in most cases they opt for an "OT" membership status. Overall the "OT" construction leads to a fundamental dilemma for the employers' associations: On the one hand it might help to stabilise their membership while on the other hand it creates an institutional legitimation for not being bound by collective agreements which in turn contributes further to the decline in bargaining coverage.

Finally, the decline in German collective bargaining has also taken place against the background of a significant weakening of trade union power resources (Dribbusch et al.

FIGURE 3

Members of the German employers' association Gesamtmetall with an "OT" membership status, 2005–2017

Percentage shares of all member companies and affected workers

— Companies   — Workers

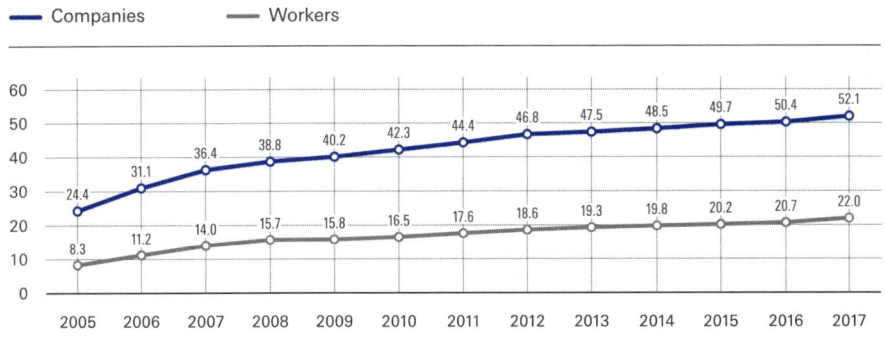

Source: Gesamtmetall; own calculation

WSI Mitteilungen

FIGURE 4

Trade union density in Germany, 1993–2016

Employed union members in per cent of all employees

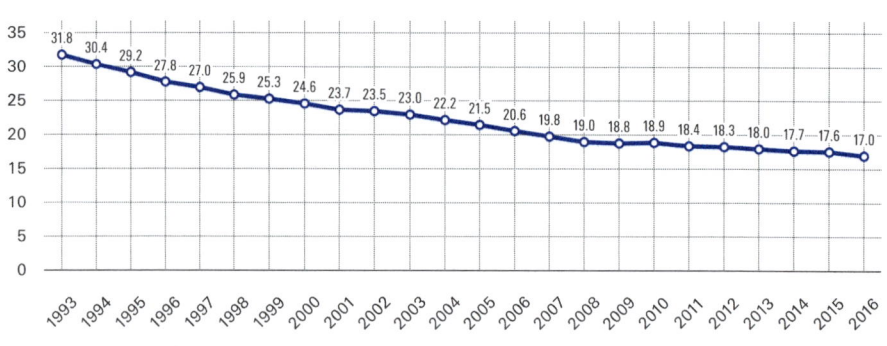

Source: OECD

WSI Mitteilungen

2018). In many cases unions just lack the organisational strength to prevent individual firms from withdrawing from collective agreements or to put pressure on non-covered firms to enter into collective bargaining. Since the early 1990s German trade unions have lost about half of their members, so that the union density decreased from 32 per cent in 1993 to around 17 per cent in 2016 *(figure 4)*.

2.3 Current Status of German Collective Bargaining

In 2017, 55 per cent of the workers were employed in a company which was bound by a collective agreement according to data provided by the IAB Establishment Panel *(figure 5)*. Among this number 47 per cent were covered by a sectoral agreement and 8 per cent by a company agreement. 45 per cent of the workers were hired in companies without binding collective agreements. In half of these cases, however, the companies claimed to take existing sectoral agreements as an "orientation" for their own in-house working arrangements, so that the influence of collective bargaining goes beyond the scope of formal bargaining coverage. The German peak employers' association BDA *(Bundesvereinigung der deutschen Arbeitgeberverbände)* even states that "80 per cent of the workers in Germany are directly or indirectly covered by collective agreements" (BDA 2018a; author's translation). All studies on that issue, however, came to the same conclusion that those companies which claim to take collective agreements as a voluntary orientation usually provide for wages and conditions well below collectively agreed standards (Addison et al. 2016; Berwing 2016; Schulten et al. 2018; Bossler 2019). Thus,

FIGURE 5

Collective bargaining coverage in Germany, 2017

Percentage shares of workers employed in companies covered by collective agreements

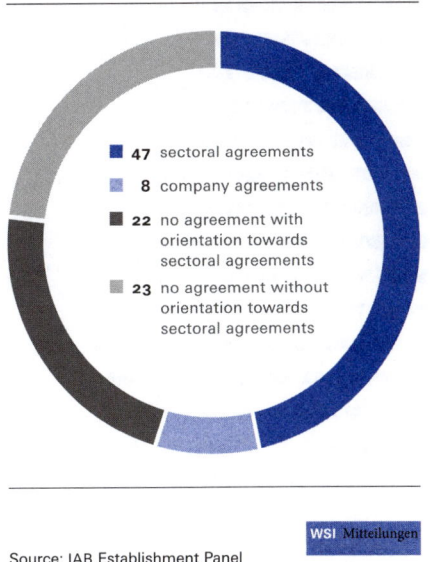

- **47** sectoral agreements
- **8** company agreements
- **22** no agreement with orientation towards sectoral agreements
- **23** no agreement without orientation towards sectoral agreements

WSI Mitteilungen

Source: IAB Establishment Panel

orientation is not at all a substitute for a formal bargaining coverage.

There are also significant differences regarding the regional and sectoral scope of collective agreements as well as regarding the different types of companies. First, there are major regional differences in the collective bargaining coverage, varying from 63 per cent in the federal state of North Rhine-Westphalia to 43 per cent in the federal state of Saxony *(figure 6)*. In general, the bargaining coverage is much lower in the east German federal states where the bargaining coverage is often below 50 per cent.

Secondly, there are also huge differences in the sectoral scope of collective agreements *(figure 7)*. In some sectors there is still a large majority of the workers hired in companies with collective agreements. This holds true in particular for public administration where almost every worker is covered by a collective agreement. Rather high coverages of 80 per cent and more also exist in the energy, water, waste disposal and mining as well as in banking and insurances. In construction and manufacturing the coverage is around 60 per cent. However, there are great differences among the different manufacturing industries. According to data provided by the German Structure of Earnings, which allow for a more precise analysis of the different sectors, in some industries such as the automotive or the chemical industry the coverage is between 60 and 70 per cent. However, in some sectors such as machine building it is 54 per cent and in the electronic industry it is only 36 per cent (Statistisches Bundesamt 2016).

Only a minority of workers are covered by collective agreements in many private services. The lowest ratio, with less than 20 per cent, can be found in the information and communication sector, followed by hotels and restaurants and wholesale and retail trade with less than 40 per cent. The structural changes in the German economy towards the service sector have been another major driver for the decline in bargaining coverage (Ellguth/Kohaut 2019). All in all, Germany is characterised by a growing fragmentation of collective bargaining among sectors (Doellgast/Greer 2007) and rather different sectoral worlds of industrial relations (Dribbusch et al. 2018; Hassel/Schroeder 2018).

FIGURE 6

Collective bargaining coverage in the German federal states, 2016

Percentage shares of workers employed in companies covered by collective agreements

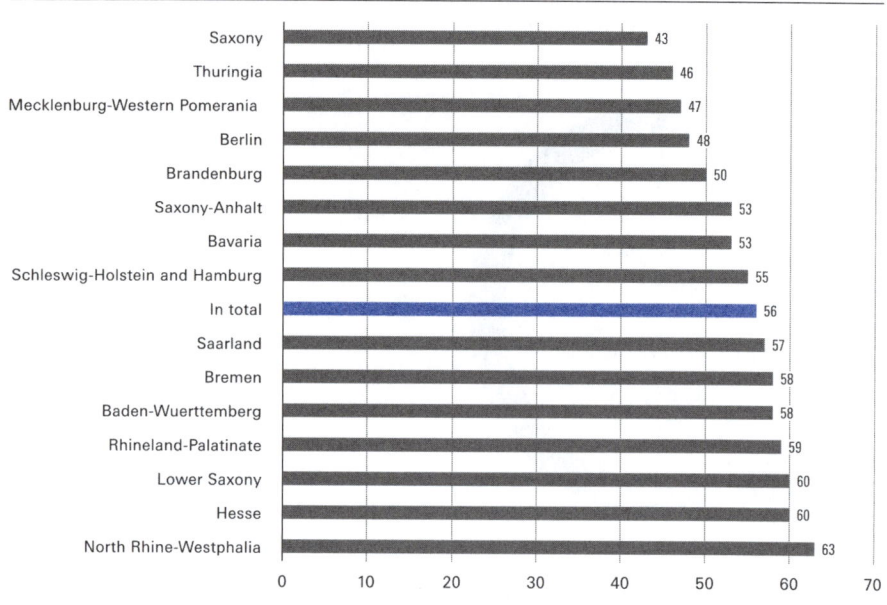

Source: IAB Establishment Panel

Finally, there is a clear correlation between the size of the establishment and the bargaining coverage *(figure 8)*. While 85 per cent of the larger establishments with 500 and more workers are covered by a collective agreement, it is only 22 per cent among smaller establishments with less than ten workers. Given the fact that the large majority of establishments are small and medium sized, on average only 29 per cent of all establishments in Germany fall under the scope of a collective agreement.

The size of the establishment also corresponds with the existence of a works council which – although it is not a trade union body – often represents *de facto* the union in the company and has the official task of providing surveillance of compliance with the collective agreements. Moreover, establishments with works councils are much more likely to be covered by a collective agreement than establishments without one (Addinson et al. 2017, Ellguth/Kohaut 2018). For the unions the works council is often the strategic actor at company level for promoting the acceptance of collective agreements.

FIGURE 7

Collective bargaining coverage in various sectors, 2017

Percentage shares of workers employed in companies covered by collective agreements

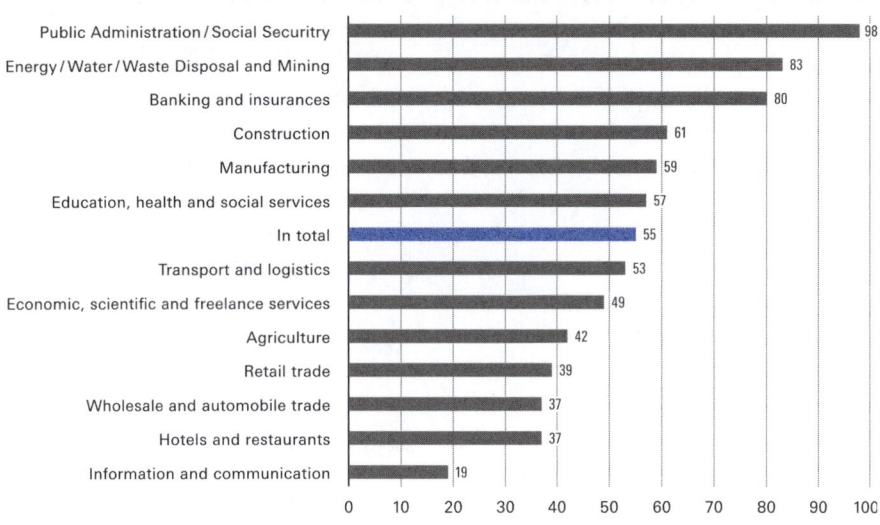

Source: IAB Establishment Panel

2.4 German Collective Bargaining Coverage in European Comparison

At the first glance bargaining coverage in Europe shows huge differences; from countries like France or Austria where almost every worker is covered by a collective agreement to countries like Bulgaria, Latvia or Lithuania where it is only a small minority of less than 15 per cent *(figure 9)*. Although all European countries are more or less faced by the same fundamental socio-economic changes, these do not automatically lead to a decline in the bargaining coverage (Visser 2013). On the contrary, there seem to be alternative development paths towards maintaining high bargaining coverage, so that it is of high importance that the reasons behind the different developments are identified.

Obviously, the differences in collective bargaining are not simply the result of differences in trade union power. For many countries the correlation between bargaining coverage and trade union density is rather weak *(figure 8)*. Among them the most extreme example is France, which has a bargaining coverage of 99 per cent while only a small minority of the workers (8 per cent) is a member of a union.

As international comparative studies have shown very clearly, the existence of a high level of bargaining coverage depends to large extent on whether or not there are efficient instruments of political support for the collective bargaining system (Visser 2013; Schulten et al. 2015; Fornasier 2017). One major instrument here is the extension of collective agreements to non-covered firms which is extensively used, for example, in countries such as Belgium, France, Spain, the Netherlands or Finland. Other instruments focus more on the strengthening of trade unions and employers' associations as organisations and therewith promote collective bargaining more indirectly. Examples for the latter are the so-called Ghent system in Belgium or the Scandinavian countries or the chamber system in Austria. In contrast to that, countries with rather low bargaining coverage are usually lacking in effective instruments of political support. This also holds true for Germa-

FIGURE 8

Collective bargaining coverage with regard to the size of the establishments, 2017

Percentage shares of companies covered by collective agreements

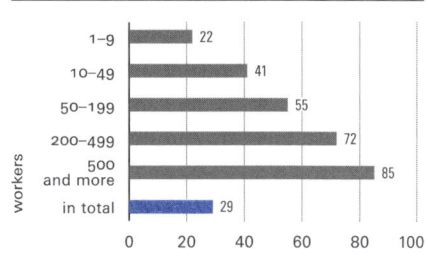

Source: IAB Establishment Panel

ny where trade unions and employers' association receive almost no organisational support while extension is rather limited to a very small number of collective agreements (Schulten 2018a).

3   Approaches for a Revitalisation of German Collective Bargaining

As the decline in bargaining coverage is still an ongoing process in Germany, the debates among trade unions, employers' associations and politicians have in recent years increasingly focused on the question of how to stop that trend and how to achieve a revitalisation of German collective bargaining. In the meantime, there are various measures and proposals under discussion, which can be summarised as three basic approaches. The first emphasises a *revitalisation from below* approach and a focusing on the re-strengthening of trade union power at company level in order to force the employers to adopt collective agreements. The second is a *revitalisation from above* approach and focuses on political support for collective bargaining, e. g. through the more frequent use of extension. Finally, a third approach, which is largely promoted by the German employers, is *revitalisation through "more flexible" agreements* which is intended to make collective bargaining more attractive to the companies.

FIGURE 9

Collective bargaining coverage and trade union density in Europe, 2016 [A]

Percentage shares of workers covered by collective agreements and members of a union

■ collective bargaining coverage   ▨ trade union density

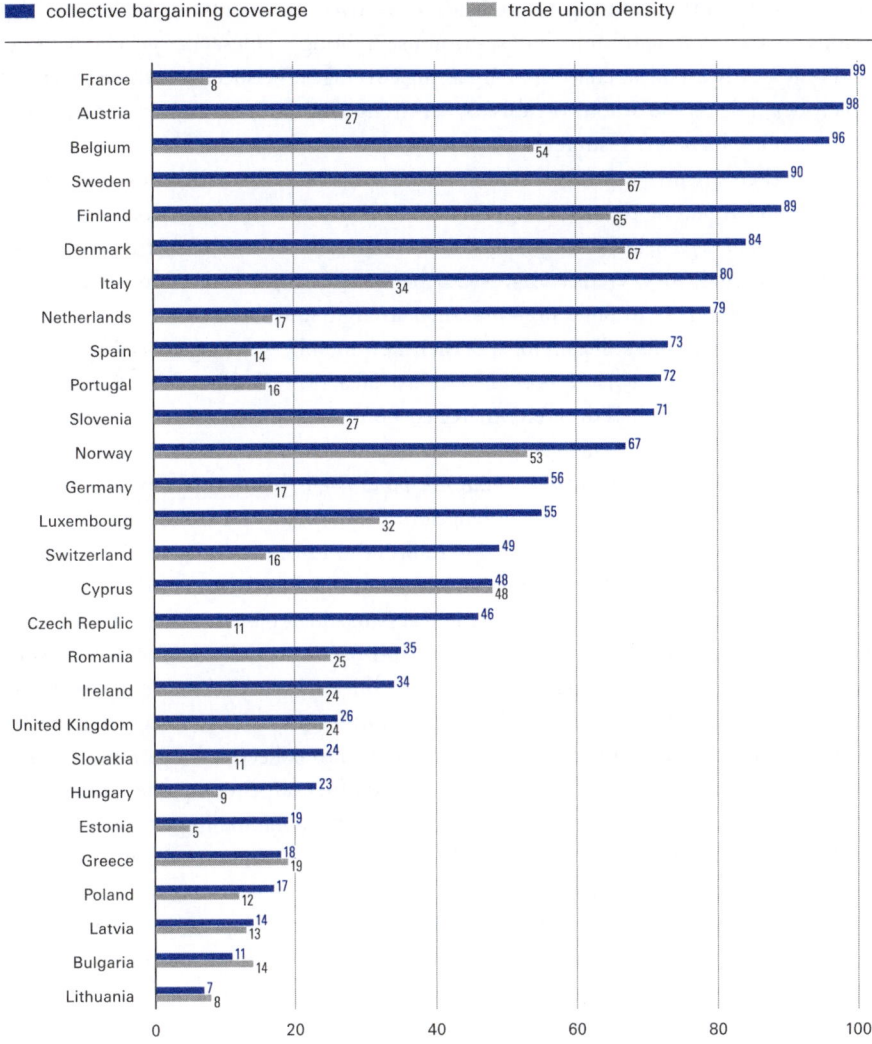

[A] or latest available figure

Source: ILO Statistics

WSI Mitteilungen

3.1 Revitalisation from Below

With the decline in bargaining coverage, German trade unions are permanently confronted either with established firms withdrawing from collective bargaining or with newly-founded firms refusing to conclude collective agreements. In both cases the unions are forced to enter into "house-to-house fighting" *(Häuserkampf)* either to defend or to newly establish collective bargaining coverage. The success of these struggles largely depends on the union's organisational strength at the company level and its ability to mobilise its power resources.

So far, there are no quantitative studies on the overall impact of this "house-to-house fighting" on bargaining coverage in Germany. However, there is a wealth of literature on the adoption of organising strategies by the German trade unions (e. g. Brinkmann et al. 2008; Kocsis et al. 2013; Wetzel 2013; Nicklich/Helfen 2019), which often show a close link between attempts to build organisational strength and the enforcing of collective agreements. The unions still gain most of their new members during collective bargaining, especially if the latter is supported by industrial action (Dribbusch 2016).

A prominent example is the e-commerce corporation Amazon, which has refused to sign any collective agreement since it started its business in Germany. The trade union responsible in this service sector is *ver.di (Vereinte Dienstleistungsgewerkschaft)* and it has tried to build up organisational strength in the company for more than five years and has frequently taken industrial action in order to force the company to accept the existing sectoral agreement for the retail trade (Boewe/Schulten 2017). While ver.di has not yet managed to get a collective agreement at Amazon, it has been more successful at the airline Ryanair, which also followed a very anti-union attitude for a long time. After the union was able to recruit many new members during industrial action, Ryanair first recognised *ver.di* as the relevant trade union and in a second move it signed an agreement in which the company obliged itself to enter into collective bargaining (Adams 2018). While the struggles at Amazon, Ryanair and other larger companies attract a lot of nation-wide attention and therewith also gain some symbolic importance, most of the "house-to-house fighting" takes place in smaller and medium-sized companies and reaches only a local or regional audience.

In recent years many German unions have tried to develop more systematic approaches to enforce collective bargaining through the build-up of new organisational strength at company level. The probably most advanced approaches have been devised by the German Metalworkers' Union *IG Metall* with the concept of so-called "development projects" *(Erschließungsprojekte)* (IG Metall Bezirk Baden-Württemberg 2018; Hassel/Schroeder 2018; Schroeder 2018). The aim of that concept is a systematic and coordinated approach to organise new companies and to bring them under the coverage of collective agreements. To this end *IG Metall* hired around 140 new organisers in order to support local development projects. Every regional and local organisation of the union is supposed to define its own development projects and can apply for support from additional organisers. The *IG Metall* district organisation of Baden-Württemberg, for example, has adopted its own target plan called "Strategy 2025" according to which every local union organisation should bring every year at least one or two new companies under the coverage of a collective agreement, so that about 100 000 additional workers (one sixth of the non-covered workforce in the region) would be covered by 2025. Since 2016, when the new project began, the union has already been able to enforce collective agreements in more than 100 additional establishments involving more than 30 000 workers (IG Metall Bezirk Baden-Württemberg 2019).

For the German unions the strengthening of their own organisational power has become the core issue and is seen at same time as the major precondition for a revitalisation of collective bargaining from below. However, the "house-to-house fighting" is a rather cost and personnel intensive approach which in many areas might run into danger of overtaxing trade union resources. The latter holds true, in particular, in sectors such as hotels and restaurants or the retail trade which are dominated by rather small companies and traditionally have low union density. Reaching a high level of bargaining coverage in these sectors not only relies on trade union power but in addition demands other forms of political support.

3.2 Revitalisation from Above

As collective agreements are not only contracts between private social actors but by regulating working conditions, additionally fulfil the function of a public good, it is also the responsibility of the state to ensure favourable conditions for collective bargaining (Schulten 2018b). In comparison with other European countries, political support for collective bargaining is not very much advanced in Germany (see section 2.3 above). Considering the historical experiences with authoritarian state interventions during the Weimar Republic and the total abolition of free collective bargaining during the Nazi period, Germany has developed a very strong notion of "collective bargaining autonomy" *(Tarifautonomie)* which for a long time has largely been understood as being free of any forms of state regulations.

With the decrease in bargaining coverage, however, the debates in Germany have started to become somewhat less idealistic and have focused more on the interrelationship between collective bargaining and state regulations. The most obvious expression of a somewhat different perception was the introduction of a statutory minimum wage in 2015 (Bosch 2018). As the latter was part of the "Law for the Strengthening of Collective Bargaining Autonomy", the statutory minimum wage has been regarded as an instrument to strengthen collective bargaining, as it establishes a general wage floor and, therewith, limits the downward pressure on collective agreements.

A more direct instrument, with which the state traditionally supports collective bargaining, is the extension of collective agreements to non-covered firms (on the following: Schulten 2018a). Since the 1950s, however, this instrument has only been used in a very small number of sectors and has continuously lost its importance, so that in recent years only less than two per cent of all sector-level collective agreements in Germany have been declared generally binding. The reasons for the very limited use of extension have been on the one hand the rather high preconditions, according to which it was necessary for the sector-level collective agreement to already cover 50 per cent of all workers in the affected bargaining area. On the other hand, every extension has to be approved by a majority of the so-called Collective Bargaining Committee *(Tarifausschuss)* at the Ministry of Labour. The Collective Bargaining Committee is composed of three representatives from each of the peak-level organisations of trade unions and employers' associations. Therewith, both parties have *de facto* a veto power and could block the extension. However, in almost all cases in which an application for the extension failed, it was the peak employers' association *BDA* which made use of that veto power.

The *BDA* has always taken a rather restrictive view of extensions, demanding that they should only be used in "exceptional cases" and should not become the rule (BDA 2018b). The *BDA* has also repeatedly blocked extensions even when they have been supported by their own sectoral member organisations (Schulten 2018a). While the employers in some sectors such as, for example, construction or security services have a rather positive attitude, the majority supports the skepticism of their peak organisation. The latter becoming reinforced after many sectoral employers' associations had introduced the "OT" membership status and therewith had established an organisational principle which fundamentally contradicted the concept of extension.

When in 2014 the German government aimed to facilitate the use of extensions, it abolished the strict 50 per cent threshold and replaced it by a vaguer provision that the collective agreement had to be of "predominant importance". Apart from that, the reform neither abolished the employer's veto power against extensions, nor did it restrict the use of "OT" membership in employers' associations. As a result, the reform largely failed to promote more extensions. Consequently, trade unions have demanded a reform to extensions by removing the remaining barriers, as, in particular, the employers' veto power (DGB 2017, Körzell/Nassibi 2017).

Another political instrument to support collective bargaining is the introduction of pay clauses *(Tariftreuevorgaben)* in public procurement and other public benefits (Schulten et al. 2012; Sack et al. 2016). The principle idea here is that public money should only be given to companies which are covered by collective agreements. During the 2000s many federal states in Germany introduced such pay clauses into their regional public procurement laws. In the late 2000s, however, the European Court of Justice (ECJ) largely restricted the use of these pay clauses as they were claimed to contravene the fundamental principle of freedom of services in the EU. In the meantime, however, new judgements issued by the ECJ, as well as new regulations at EU level, have again widened the possibilities of using public contracts to promote collective bargaining.

There are various other instruments in the debate on how the state might support the bargaining system (DGB 2017). One is the improvement of the so-called after-effect *(Nachwirkung)* of collective agreements, aimed at making it less attractive for companies to withdraw from collective bargaining. Another instrument under discussion is the more widespread use of optional provisions which allow a divergence from labour law via collective agreements *(tarifdispositive Regelungen)*. Such provisions already exist in a small number of laws (Deutscher Bundestag 2017), but have had no major effects on collective bargaining so far. One exemption is the law on temporary agency work, where a provision allows collective agreements to diverge from the equal treatment principle and therewith has promoted almost 100 per cent bargaining coverage in that sector. For the unions, however, this provision creates the paradox situation that collective agreements *de facto* worsen the legal situation. The unions have therefore decided in future to accept such provisions only if diverging regulations are equivalent to the legal conditions (DGB 2017).

Finally, there have been some recent debates on whether tax reductions could help to promote collective bargaining. One concrete proposal is the introduction of a tax exemption for trade union members in companies covered by collective agreements (Franzen 2018). Another proposal by the German Minister of Labour was the introduction of tax bonuses for companies with collective agreements (Handelsblatt, 13 December 2018). To sum up, there is a growing belief that the state should no longer accept the ongoing decline in bargaining coverage and should use political instruments to reverse that trend.

3.3 Revitalisation through More Flexible Agreements

In contrast to the unions, most of the German employers' associations still refuse to accept any political intervention into collective bargaining. They emphasise that the application of collective agreements has to be voluntary and refer to the so-called "negative freedom of association". Moreover, they even have an interest that not all companies are covered by collective agreements as the competitive pressure from the non-covered sector might strengthen the employers' position in collective bargaining (Lesch et al. 2017b).

For the employers' associations the only way to increase the level of bargaining coverage is to conclude "better agreements" (Kramer 2018). According to a recent survey among employers in the German metal industry, there is significant dissatisfaction with existing collective agreements especially in the area of working time but also regarding the level of payments (Lesch et al. 2018). In order to increase the acceptance of collective agreements among firms, the employers' associations demand not only the introduction of more opening clauses but more fundamentally they propose a "modularisation of collective agreements" (Dulger 2018; Kramer 2018). According to the latter, employers should no longer be obliged to fulfil the whole collective agreement but should have the opportunity to choose only those "modules" of the agreements which they find applicable. The pattern for such flexible agreements should be those firms which are today not formally covered by collective agreements but use existing agreements as an "orientation".

For the unions, however, such proposals are far from being acceptable as the proposed "modularisation" would lead to a hollowing out of the substance of a collective agreement. It is also extremely doubtful that more flexible agreements would lead to higher bargaining coverage as in the end the most flexible companies are always those companies which are not covered by any agreements at all. Finally, the developments of the past two decades have shown very clearly that although collective bargaining has become much more flexible with opening clauses in all major agreements, this could not avoid the ongoing decline in the level of bargaining coverage (Schulten/Bispinck 2018).

4 Outlook: What Future for German Collective Bargaining?

In a speech to a trade union congress in 2017 the German Chancellor Angela Merkel said: "I will do everything I can to increase collective bargaining coverage in Germany" (Merkel 2017). After more than two decades of erosion collective bargaining in Germany has reached a point where all relevant social actors recognise that "something has to be done" in order to stabilise the system. However, there are still differing views regarding the right measures and instruments necessary for revitalisation.

For the unions, the first priority is to regain organisational power within the company, which is seen as a major precondition to securing collective bargaining. In recent years there have been hundreds of cases where employers have not been willing to enter into collective bargaining as long as they had not received significant pressure from the unions. For this reason, organising projects are often closely linked with struggles for the enforcement of works councils and collective agreements.

As experiences from Anglo-Saxon countries have shown very clearly, however, an exclusive focus on organising might lead to important successes in enforcing collective agreements at company level, but largely fail to increase overall bargaining coverage. Comprehensive bargaining coverage can only be reached by a system of sector-level agreements which, apart from strong organisations, usually also require forms of political support. Therefore, the demands of German unions are for various political measures which would strengthen collective bargaining and these demands seem to be increasingly reaching the ears of the political actors.

Finally, a key question for the future of German collective bargaining is the further development of the employers' associations which have manoeuvered themselves into a fundamental dilemma as their organisational strength depends more and more on the "OT" membership status which at the same time significantly weakens collective bargaining. To overcome this dilemma, they need other forms of organisational support as, for example, a more widespread use of extensions which in other European countries have contributed to strengthening both the employers' associations as well as the bargaining coverage. Therefore, it would be in the employer's own interest to give up their resistance to any form of state support for collective bargaining.

REFERENCES

Adams, C. (2018): Ryanair strike: Airline signs agreement with German cabin crew union, in: The Independent, 9 November 2018

Addison, J. / Teixeira, P. / Evers, K. / Bellmann, L. (2016): Is the erosion thesis overblown? Alignment from without in Germany, in: Industrial Relations 55 (3), pp. 415–443

Addison, J. / Teixeira, P. / Pahnke, A. / Bellmann, L. (2017): The demise of a model? The state of collective bargaining and worker representation in Germany, in: Economic and Industrial Democracy 38 (2), pp. 193–234

BDA (Bundesvereinigung der deutschen Arbeitgeberverbände) (2018a): Tarifautonomie, BDA kompakt, Berlin, https://www.arbeitgeber.de/www/arbeitgeber.nsf/res/EB5916A000F 715CEC1257E8C002013FF/$file/kompakt-Tarifautonomie.pdf

BDA (2018b): Allgemeinverbindlicherklärung von Tarifverträgen, BDA kompakt, Berlin, https://www.arbeitgeber.de/www/arbeitgeber.nsf/res/581BD968A0F6E367C12574EB004BCA0F/$file/kompakt_ave.pdf

Behrens, M. / Helfen, M. (2016): Sachzwang oder Programm? Tarifpolitische Orientierungen und OT-Mitgliedschaft bei deutschen Arbeitgeberverbänden, in: WSI-Mitteilungen 69 (6), pp. 452–459

Behrens. M. / Helfen, M. (2019): Small change, big impact? Organisational membership rules and the exit of employers' associations from multiemployer bargaining in Germany, in: Human Resource Management Journal 29 (1), pp. 51–66

Berwing, S. (2016): Tariforientierung in Deutschland – zwischen Tariflandschaft und Tarifödnis, Schriften der Forschungsstelle für Betriebswirtschaft und Sozialpraxis (FBS), Mannheim

Bispinck, R. / Dribbusch, H. / Schulten, T. (2010): German collective bargaining in a European perspective. Continuous erosion or re-stabilisation of multi-employer agreements?, Wirtschafts- und Sozialwissenschaftliches Institut (WSI) in der HBS: Discussion Paper No. 171, Düsseldorf, https://www.boeckler.de/pdf/p_wsi_diskp_171.pdf

Boewe, J. / Schulten, J. (2017): The long struggle of the Amazon employees, Rosa Luxemburg Foundation, Brussels Office, https://www.rosalux.eu/fileadmin/user_upload/Publications/2017/Long-struggle-of-Amazon-employees.pdf

Bosch, G. (2018): The making of the German minimum wage: a case study of institutional change, in: Industrial Relations Journal 49 (1), pp. 19–33

Bossler, M. (2019): The rise in orientation at collective bargaining without a formal contract, in: Industrial Relations 58 (1), pp. 17–45

Brinkmann, U. / Choi, H. / Detje, R. / Dörre, K. / Holst, H. / Karakayali, S. / Schmalstieg, C. (2008): Strategic Unionism: Aus der Krise zur Erneuerung?, Wiesbaden

Deutscher Bundestag (2017): Tarifdispositives Arbeitsrecht. Ausgewählte Beispiele. Untersuchung des wissenschaftlichen Dienstes des Bundestages, WD 6 -3000 -138/16, https://www.bundestag.de/blob/495532/afb9650158fc29cd3b8cb42a01b4cdd8/wd-6-138-16-pdf-data.pdf

DGB (Deutscher Gewerkschaftsbund) (2017): Positionen zur Stärkung der Tarifbindung, Berlin, 28 February 2017, http://www.dgb.de/themen/++co++dfdaadb8-ff1f-11e6-a620-525400e5a74a

Doellgast, V. / Greer, I. (2007): Vertical disintegration and the disorganization of German industrial relations, in: British Journal of Industrial Relations 45 (1), pp. 55–76

Dribbusch, H. (2016): Organizing through conflict: exploring the relationship between strikes and union membership in Germany, in: Transfer. European Review of Labour and Research 22 (3), pp. 347–365

Dribbusch, H. / Lehndorff, S. / Schulten, T. (2018): Two worlds of unionism? German manufacturing and service unions since the Great Recession, in: Lehndorff, S. / Dribbusch, H. / Schulten, T. (eds.): Rough waters. European trade unions in a time of crises, 2nd revised ed., Brussels, pp. 209–233

Dulger, R. (2018): 100 Jahre Stinnes-Legien-Abkommen. Speech at the Gesamtmetall conference on „Die Zukunft der Tarifautonomie in Deutschland", Berlin, 21 November 2018, https://www.gesamt metall.de/sites/default/files/downloads/rede_gesamtmetall_praesident_dulger_zu_100_jahre_stinnes_legien.pdf

Ellguth, P. / Kohaut, S. (2010): Auf der Flucht? Tarifaustritte und die Rolle von Öffnungsklauseln, in: Industrielle Beziehungen 17 (4), pp. 345–371

Ellguth, P. / Kohaut, S. (2018): Tarifbindung und betriebliche Interessenvertretung. Ergebnisse aus dem IAB-Betriebspanel 2017, in: WSI-Mitteilungen 71 (4), pp. 299–306

Ellguth, P. / Kohaut, S. (2019): A Note on the decline of collective bargaining coverage: the role of structural change, in: Jahrbücher für Nationalökonomie und Statistik 239 (1), pp. 39–66

Flecker, J. / Schulten, T. (1999): The end of institutional stability: What Future for the "German Model"?, in: Economic & Industrial Democracy 20 (1), pp. 81–115

Franzen, M. (2018): Stärkung der Tarifautonomie durch Anreize zum Verbandsbeitritt, Hugo-Sinzheimer-Institut (HSI): HSI-Schriftenreihe Vol. 27, Frankfurt a. M.

Fornasier, M. (2017): Wege zur Stärkung der Tarifbindung – ein rechtsvergleichender Streifzug zur Untersuchung funktionaler Äquivalente der Allgemeinverbindlicherklärung von Tarifverträgen, in: Soziales Recht 6/2017, pp. 239–254

Hassel, A. (1999): The erosion of the German system of industrial relations, in: British Journal of Industrial Relations 37 (3), pp. 483–505

Hassel, A. / Schroeder, W. (2018): Gewerkschaften 2030. Rekrutierungsdefizite, Repräsentationslücken und neue Strategien der Mitgliederpolitik, Wirtschafts- und Sozialwissenschaftliches Institut (WSI) in der HBS: WSI-Report No. 44, Düsseldorf, https://www.boeckler.de/pdf/p_wsi_report_44_2018.pdf

Hassel, A. / Schulten, T. (1998): Globalization and the future of central collective bargaining: the example of the German metal industry, in: Economy and Society 27 (4), pp. 484–522

Hayter, S. (2015): Unions and collective bargaining, in: Berg, J. (ed.): Labour markets, institutions and inequality, Cheltenham/Geneva, pp. 95–122

IG Metall Bezirk Baden-Württemberg (ed.) (2018): Aufrecht gehen. Wie beschäftigte durch Organizing zu ihrem Recht kommen, Hamburg

IG Metall Bezirk Baden-Württemberg (2019): IG Metall Baden-Württemberg wächst auf über 441.000 Mitglieder – Neue Kampagne zur Tarifbindung startet, Press Release, 21 January 2019

Kocsis, A. / Sterkel, G. / Wiedemuth, J. (eds.) (2013): Organisieren am Konflikt. Tarifauseinandersetzungen und Mitgliederentwicklung im Dienstleistungssektor, Hamburg

Kohaut, S. (2018): Binding collective agreements. The downward trend continues, IAB-Forum, https://www.iab-forum.de/en/binding-collective-agreements-the-downward-trend-continues/?pdf=8008

Körzell, S. / Nassibi, G. (2017): Zukunftsfragen der Tarifpolitik am Beispiel der Allgemeinverbindlicherklärung aus Sicht des DGB, in: Schulten, T. / Dribbusch, H. / Bäcker, G. / Klenner, C. (eds.): Tarifpolitik als Gesellschaftspolitik. Strategische Herausforderungen im 21. Jahrhundert, Hamburg, pp. 234–243

Kramer, I. (2018): Mehr Tarifbindung nur mit neuer Tarifpolitik!, in: Frankfurter Allgemeine Zeitung, 11 October 2018

Lehndorff S. / Bosch G. / Haipeter T. / Latniak, E. (2009): From the "sick man" to the "overhauled engine" of Europe? Upheaval in the German model, in: Bosch G. / Lehndorff S. / Rubery J. (eds.): European employment models in flux: a comparison of institutional change in nine European countries, Basingstoke, pp. 105–131

Lesch, H. / Vogel, S. / Hellmich. P. (2017a): The state and social partners working together: Germany's response to the global financial and economic crisis, ILO Working Paper, Geneva

Lesch, H. / Vogel, S. / Busshoff, H. / Giza, A. (2017b): Stärkung der Tarifbindung, Institut der Deutschen Wirtschaft (IW): IW-Analysen Nr. 120, Cologne

Lesch, H. / Schneider, H. / Vogel, S. (2018): Rückzug aus der Flächentarifbindung: empirischer Forschungsstand und Implikationen für eine Stabilisierung des Tarifsystems, in: Sozialer Fortschritt 67 (10), pp. 867–886

Merkel, A. (2017): Speech at the 6th Congress of the Mining, Chemical and Energy Workers Union (IG BCE) on 12 October 2017 in Hannover, https://www.bundesregierung.de/breg-de/service/bulletin/rede-von-bundeskanzlerin-dr-angela-merkel-787296

Nicklich, M. / Helfen, M. (2019): Trade union renewal and "organizing from below" in Germany: Institutional constraints, strategic dilemmas and organizational tensions, in: European Journal of Industrial Relations 25 (1), pp. 57–73

Oberfichtner, M. / Schnabel, C. (2017): The German model of industrial relations: (Where) Does it still exist?, Institute of Labor Economics (ISA): IZA Discussion Paper No. 11064, Bonn, http://ftp.iza.org/dp11064.pdf

Sack, D. / Schulten, T. / Sarter, E. K. / Böhlke, N. (2016): Öffentliche Auftragsvergabe in Deutschland. Sozial und nachhaltig?, Baden-Baden

Schneider, H. / Vogel, S. (2018): Tarifbindung der Beschäftigten in Deutschland. Eine Auswertung des Sozioökonomischen Panels, Institut der Deutschen Wirtschaft (IW): IW-Report No. 15, Cologne

Schroeder, W. (2018): Strategien der Tarifvertragsparteien zur Stärkung ihrer Mitgliederbasis, in: Sozialer Fortschritt 67 (10), pp. 887–906

Schulten, T. (2018a): The role of extension in German collective bargaining, in: Hayter, S. / Visser, J. (eds.): Collective agreements: Extending labour protection, Geneva, pp. 65–92

Schulten, T. (2018b): Zur Aktualität historischer Debatten im Kontext der Tarifvertragsordnung von 1918, in: Sozialer Fortschritt 67 (10), pp. 849–865

Schulten, T. / Bispinck, R. (2018): Varieties of decentralisation in German collective bargaining, in: Leonardi, S. / Perdersini, R. (eds.): Multi-employer bargaining under pressure. Decentralisation trends in five European countries, Brussels, pp. 105–149

Schulten, T. / Alsos, K. / Burgess, P. / Pedersen, K. (2012): Pay and other clauses in the European public procurement. An overview on regulation and practices with a focus on Denmark, Germany, Norway, Switzerland and the United Kingdom. Study on behalf of the European Federation of Public Service Unions (EPSU), Düsseldorf, https://www.epsu.org/article/pay-and-other-social-clauses-european-public-procurement

Schulten, T. / Eldring, L. / Naumann, R. (2015): The role of extension for the strength and stability of collective bargaining in Europe, in: Van Gyes, G. / Schulten, T. (eds.): Wage bargaining under the new European Economic Governance, Brussels, pp. 361–400

Schulten, T. / Lübker, M. / Bispinck, R. (2018): Tarifverträge und Tarifflucht in Bayern, Wirtschafts- und Sozialwissenschaftliches Institut (WSI) in der HBS: WSI Study No. 13, Düsseldorf, https://www.boeckler.de/pdf/p_wsi_studies_13_2018.pdf

Statistisches Bundesamt (2016): Tarifbindung in Deutschland 2014, Wiesbaden, https://www.destatis.de/DE/Publikationen/Thematisch/VerdiensteArbeitskosten/Tarifverdienste/Tarifbindung5622103149004.pdf?__blob=publicationFile

Streeck, W. (2009): Re-forming capitalism. Institutional change in the German political economy, Oxford

Urban, H.-J. (2013): Vom Krisen- zum Strategieparadigma? Argumente für eine Neuausrichtung der deutschen Gewerkschaftsforschung, in: Urban, H.-J.: Der Tiger und seine Dompteure. Wohlfahrtsstaat und Gewerkschaften im Gegenwartskapitalismus, Hamburg, pp. 161–175

Visser, J. (2013): Wage bargaining institutions – from crisis to crisis, European Commission: European Economy. Economic Papers 488, Brussels, http://ec.europa.eu/economy_finance/publications/economic_paper/2013/pdf/ecp488_en.pdf

Wetzel, D. (ed.) (2013): Organizing. Die Veränderung der gewerkschaftlichen Praxis durch das Prinzip Beteiligung, Hamburg

AUTHOR

THORSTEN SCHULTEN, Prof. Dr., is Senior Researcher at the Institute of Economic and Social Research (WSI) within the Hans-Böckler-Foundation in Düsseldorf, Germany. Main areas of research: WSI company agreements archive, labour and collective bargaining policy.

@ E-Mail: Thorsten-Schulten@boeckler.de

Avoiding the Union at the Workplace

Evidence from Surveys amongst German Trade Unions

Employer resistance to works councils is not a phenomenon that has been closely associated with German labour relations. While classic studies characterise the "German model" in terms of social partnership, more recent accounts seem to observe more diverse practices. Based on data provided by the WSI survey of paid union representatives (2012, 2015), this article investigates employer practices to obstruct or inhibit the election of works councils and analyses the diffusion of such strategies at the establishment level.

MARTIN BEHRENS, HEINER DRIBBUSCH

1 Introduction

The German system of industrial relations is commonly not associated with widespread union busting as is for example the US system (cf. Logan 2006). Quite the contrary, Germany is known rather for its fairly collaborative (social partnership-style) labour relations (Turner 1998; Behrens/Helfen 2016). However, even at its heyday this picture of the so-called "German model" was never complete and had glossed over the still existing elements of disruption and conflict (Müller-Jentsch 1993; Streeck 2016). Even within a picture of orderly and collaborative industrial relations, union organising interferes in the power relationship between labour and capital. It is for that reason that collective bargaining and the building of a meaningful union presence at the workplace has always been contested by employers.

The anti-union strategies of employers in Germany have different targets and perhaps reach less frequently the public sphere but they share with Anglo-Saxon anti-unionism two intertwined strategic goals: to prevent or weaken union power at the workplace and to avoid collective bargaining. State interferences in order to weaken unions is less prominent than for example in the US or in the UK although there have been pieces of legislation which could be considered as a weakening of unions. Our focus is on the actions of employers which have as their aim the obstruction of the establishment of a works council or, in the case where a works council exists, to threaten its existence. The establishment of a works council draws the particular attention of employers because the establishment of such a body is in most cases a corner stone to building a sustainable union presence at the workplace. Preventing the election of a works council helps to avoid the union.

However, not every case of an establishment without a works council constitutes a case of active anti-unionism to be considered in this chapter. We assume that an unknown but probably significant number of workplaces remain without workplace representation because neither a trade union nor a relevant number of employees ever made an attempt to establish one. Furthermore, even within the framework of industrial relations, which favours cooperative mechanisms of conflict resolution, substantial discrepancies between the interests of employers and unions remain. Unions can and will not expect all employers to support or even encourage workplace representation or collective bargaining. Therefore, it is not the general attitude of employers towards unions we look at but the extent of deliberate targeted action against works councils.

While there is the danger of overstating the true extent of anti-unionism by mistaking the mere absence of unions as a proxy for union avoidance we are aware that at the opposite end we might underestimate the true extent of anti-unionism because of inherent data problems. There are case studies (cf. Dribbusch 2003) and plenty of anecdotal evidence that employers create an anti-union climate at the workplace by way of "subtle", less confrontational tactics. The underlying message to employees in those establishments is that collective representation is an unnecessary interference of third parties in the relationship between employer and employee and that union membership and even more so the establishment of a works council will be considered by management as an unfriendly if not hostile act. Union membership is an impediment to internal promotion and so on. The scope and effects of these various kinds of subtle forms of "daily anti-unionism" are very difficult to measure and must be left here to future research.

In our account on employer resistance to works councils we will address three general questions: By firstly analysing the degree to which anti-union practices have already diffused within the German system of labour relations, we shall ask if employer resistance to works councils is a marginal footnote in an ocean of still collaborative labour relations or can it be seen as an indicator of an ongoing process of the erosion of the social partnership. Secondly, we look whether we detect certain patterns of anti-union activity and the degree to which anti-union behaviour is concentrated in certain types of establishments. Finally we want to briefly assess whether the extent of reported anti-union activity by employers is linked to proactive union efforts to fill the representation gap and that the non-reporting of such incidents might be due to the simple fact that the local union in place did not push for the establishment of works councils.

By focusing on strategic interactions between labour and employers at the establishment level, we seek to fill a void within the literature in the field of comparative political economy and labour relations which have predominately focused on national political coalitions and certain lead industries (see Doellgast et al. 2018).

2 The Dual System of Interest Representation

The most characteristic feature of the institutional framework of industrial relations in Germany is the "dual system of interest representation" based on trade unions and employers who are solely responsible for collective bargaining and the works council *(Betriebsrat)* as the legal body for the representation of employees at the workplace (cf. Müller-Jentsch/Weitbrecht 2003).

Collective bargaining is governed by the Collective Agreement Act *(Tarifvertrags-gesetz)* (Kempen/Zachert 2006) which was first introduced in the British and American occupation zones of post-war Germany in 1949. The Act states that only trade unions have the right to conclude collective agreements. On the employers' side, the Collective Agreement Act provides that collective agreements may be concluded either by employers' associations or by individual employers. In practice, however, Germany has seen the development of a comprehensive system of sectoral collective bargaining. Bargaining between unions and employers' associations is still the dominant pattern although company-level collective agreements *(Haustarifverträge)* have gained importance since the 1990s. Collective agreements are legally binding and enforceable. They legally apply to those signatory to the agreement; that is the individual members of the trade union and the affiliates of the employers' association concerned. In practice, however, employers usually apply the provisions of a collective agreement to all employees of a given establishment in order to avoid an incentive to join the union.

Works councils are confined to the private sector.[1] They are governed by the Works Constitution Act *(Betriebsverfassungsgesetz, BetrVG)* which was first introduced in 1952 and substantially amended in 1972 and 2001. Works councils shall be elected in all establishments that normally have five or more permanent employees. A works council is explicitly not a trade union body but represents all employees of an establishment regardless of a union membership. All employees who are 18 years of age or older have the right to vote. If they are employed for at least six months they are eligible.

The works council has a number of information, consultation and co-determination rights but neither the right to conclude collective agreements nor to call industrial action. Members of works councils enjoy legal protection against dismissal and must be provided with adequate facilities to fulfil their tasks and duties. They have substantial rights to be released from work. In workplaces with 200 or more employees, one or more members of the works councils are even entitled to be fully seconded from work. All costs ensuing from the work carried out by the works councils have to be borne by the employer.

---

1   Employee representation in the public sector at federal, federal state (Länder) or municipal level takes the form of a so-called "staff representation" *(Personalvertretung)*. These bodies have somewhat different rights than works councils and are legally governed by Staff Representation Acts at federal and Länder level.

Although not a trade union body, works councils are involved in many ways with the power relationship at the workplace. The close connection between trade unions and works councils results from the fact that the vast majority of elected works councillors are union members. In 2014, the latest election for which figures are available so far, about three quarters of members of works councils were members of a union affiliated to the German Confederation of Trade Unions *(Deutscher Gewerkschaftsbund, DGB)* (Greifenstein et al. 2017), the largest union confederation in Germany with almost 6 million members by the end of 2018. The organised members of a works council are also frequently involved in the decision making and collective bargaining processes of their respective union. Furthermore, one of the legal tasks of works councils is to ensure that collective agreements are followed by the employer. Last but not least, works council members have an important role in the day-to-day organising of new members for the union and are therefore crucial for building a sustained union presence at the workplace (Dribbusch 2003).

The initiative to establish a works council can directly come from employees. The involvement of the union is not required but in many cases employees will seek union support. A very important provision of the Works Constitution Act is to allow for the conclusion of a collective agreement (a so-called §-3-Tarifvertrag) to define constituencies of works councils which combine different establishments within one company. This is of particular importance in industries like retail. In the absence of such an agreement employees and unions are forced to organise separate elections for each outlet. Some outlets might even not qualify for a works council because they do not meet the minimum threshold of five employees.

Trade unions have a legal right of access to the premises of any establishment they are represented in. In the event of this representation being challenged by the employer, the trade union must give legal proof of having at least one member within the establishment, without, however, having to disclose the identity of the member to the employer. The Works Constitution Act gives trade unions represented in the establishment certain rights in the legal procedure to establish a works council. They can initiate the procedure and they are entitled to submit lists of candidates for the works council elections.

2.1 The Spread of Works Councils

Although being one of the best-known features of German industrial relations, works councils are rare. Data provided by the Establishment Panel of the Institute for Employment Research (IAB) of the Federal Employment Agency *(Bundesagentur für Arbeit)* indicates that in 2017 only a small minority of 9 % of establishments legally entitled to have a works council actually had one (Ellguth/Kohaut 2018). This low level of works councils is three percentage points down from 1996 figures (see *table 1*). While in 1996 at least in west Germany a small majority of 51 % of employees in the private sector were still covered by a works council this figure had dropped to 40 % by 2017. In the same year in east Germany the works council coverage of employees was even down to 33 %.

TABLE 1

Coverage of works councils according to establishment and employees, 1996 and 2017

Percentage shares

Year	Establishments[A] with a works council		Employees covered by a works council	
	West Germany	East Germany	West Germany	East Germany
1996	12	11	51	43
2017	9	9	40	33

A Establishments in private sector with five or more employees
(excluding those in agriculture and non-profit sectors)

Source: Ellguth/Kohaut 2018, p. 303, based on IAB Establishment Panel

The size of the establishment matters a great deal which explains why the share of employees covered is still significantly higher than the coverage rate of establishments. While works councils are seldom found in the great number of small workplaces, they are almost the rule in the larger ones (see *table 2*). Of the establishments with 501 and more employees, 86 % had such a body in 2017 while this applied to only 5 % of those in the size band of 5 to 50 employees.

TABLE 2

Coverage of works councils according to size of establishment, 2017

Percentage shares

	Size band (number of employees)				
	5–50	51–100	101–199	200–500	501+
Establishments[A] with works council	5	32	53	69	80
Employees covered	9	33	55	70	86

A Establishments in private sector with five or more employees
(excluding those in agriculture and non-profit sectors)

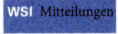

Source: Ellguth/Kohaut 2018, p. 303, based on IAB Establishment Panel

3 Union Avoidance at the Workplace

Given the crucial role of the works councils for building and sustaining a union presence, employer opposition to the establishment of such a body is the major form of union avoidance at workplace level in Germany. However, not every case of an establishment without a works council might constitute a case of active anti-unionism. We assume that a significant number of workplaces remain without workplace representation or collective bargaining because neither employees nor a union ever made an attempt to establish one. This seems particularly likely in small and very small enterprises. As the great proportion of larger establishments with works councils show, employers can accommodate workplace representation and particularly in larger companies they do so.

A major reason why there are so few works councils in small and medium-sized establishments is that the resources of unions are limited. As trade unions in Germany almost exclusively rely on membership contributions, the material and personal resources are directly linked to the number of members a union has. The limitation of resources simply does not allow all eligible establishments to be tackled. Therefore local unions will have to set priorities.

In the case of small owner-operated establishments the union will decide in each case whether it has the resources to get involved and weigh the chances of being successful. As a rule a union will not become actively involved in establishing a works council unless there is an initiative by employees who have at least some backing amongst the workforce. Local officials frequently require a certain minimum level of membership before support is given. If this is not the case they must at least be convinced that the activists approaching the union will stay firm in the face of possible employer resistance. Exceptions are made if strategically important or large workplaces are concerned.

From an employer's perspective a works council can be beneficial because it mediates in the inherent conflicts of the employment relationship. However, in interviews with managers of companies without a works council Böhm and Lücking (2006, p. 113) have also identified three motivations of employers to consider works councils as a threat, or at least a non-productive institution leading sometimes to violent rejection of this institution (ibid., p. 108). Firstly, the works council is considered to be unnecessary because there is a feeling that employees could raise their grievances on their own and management would handle these better than a works council could do. Secondly, the works council is seen as a threat to social peace because it represents egocentric or ideologically motivated interests. Finally, there is a feeling that the works council would be too costly because of the direct expenses involved, as well as the indirect costs caused by the negotiation processes involved. This widespread negative attitude towards the works council amongst managers can be based on more "traditional authoritarian" motives as well as on "modern" human resource management concepts.

Conflicts about works councils are a special case because they involve a confrontation between the employer and individual employees; they are much more personalised than, for example, disputes about collective bargaining. Candidates, even when backed by the union, remain necessarily also employees who are more or less sensitive to individual pressure or material persuasion. This personalisation offers opportunities of intervention for the employer which are largely absent in confrontations with the union as a bargaining party (Bormann 2007, p. 17). Although the Works Constitution Act (section 119) provides for penalties when there is obstruction to the establishment of works councils and even the interference of employers in works council elections, it is very rare that those cases come to the courts or that any fines or sentences are imposed (ibid., p. 21).

Many of such incidents have been researched in the retail sector, with leading grocery or drugstore chains having aggressively resisted the election of works councils (Küppers 2012; Bormann 2007; Köhnen 2006; Huhn 2001; Wohland 1995). The retail industry is a particular case in so far as big corporate organisations control a vast number of small workplaces. They quite frequently choose a form of organisation which splits the retail corporation into very small legal entities which makes the establishment of works councils particularly difficult. According to estimates by United Services Union, ver.di, in 2015 the large German food retailer EDEKA had outsourced many of its outlets to about 6000 independent retailers frequently running more than one medium-sized supermarket. Of these SMEs only between 60 and 120 were estimated to have bargaining coverage and a works council (ver.di Bundeskongress 2015, p. 65).

However, it is rather difficult to assess the full extent of employer resistance to works councils. The establishment of a works council is not an activity which is officially registered or recorded. Therefore there is neither data on the number of attempts to establish a works council, nor on how many of those attempts were effectively defeated. Even less are we able to assess in how many establishments employees feel discouraged to even start such an attempt due to perceived employer hostility.

Neither can the unions provide quantitative data about employer opposition to works councils as they do not keep appropriate records. The latest quantitative data we are aware of is based on a works council survey carried out by a regional body of the DGB which dates back to the year 1982. At that time 10 % of the works councils surveyed reported attempts made by employers to influence works council elections and 3.5 % knew of attempts to obstruct the establishment of a works council (Bormann 2007, p. 20f.). Given that the issue of employer resistance to works councils might be considered by the general public to be a rather delicate one, a potential research design which is based on information provided by those employers can hardly be feasible. An alternative design might be based on a survey of works councils who are asked to identify whether their employer has tried to obstruct the election of this representative body. But this research strategy would face a severe problem, too: If an employer is successful in obstructing the election of a works council, there would not be a respondent available for the survey.

4 The WSI Survey

Given the difficulty in collecting quantitative data, we have decided in favour of a third research strategy: In order to collect up-to-date data on employer anti-unionism we have approached several DGB-affiliated unions with a proposal to conduct a survey amongst local full-time officers. The aim was to investigate the extent to which local union bodies have knowledge of management strategies directed against works councils. A first study had been conducted in 2012 (for results of this first study see Behrens/Dribbusch 2014). In the following we report the results of a follow-up survey which had been conducted in 2015. Four unions – the German metalworkers' union *Industriegewerkschaft Metall (IG Metall)*, the chemical and mineworkers' union *Industriegewerkschaft Bergbau, Chemie, Energie (IG BCE)*, the food and restaurant workers' union *Gewerkschaft Nahrung-Genuss-Gaststätten (NGG)* and the United Services Union *Vereinte Dienstleistungsgewerkschaft (ver.di)* – agreed to participate in the study. While the data collection within the first three unions ran smoothly, it proved to be extremely difficult to collect data within ver.di as they have a particularly complicated organisational structure. The union is divided into 13 trade groups which each had units in the 80 local districts (as of 2015) of the union. After we had learned from our first survey that a general top-down approach within ver.di failed to deliver a relevant number of responses, we agreed with the union to concentrate on three of their 13 trade groups: retail and wholesale trades, postal services and logistics and special services *(Besondere Dienstleistungen)*, the latter being an umbrella for various service branches ranging from private security to facility management.

Together with the participating unions we developed and later refined a brief questionnaire with a variety of questions concerning management hostility towards works councils. In the first section we asked local full-time officials whether they were aware of attempts by management to obstruct the establishment of works councils. If this was the case, we further asked details about specific cases. In order to reduce the risk of non-response we restricted these more detailed questions to a maximum of five in each unit. In a second part of the survey we investigated measures taken against already existing works council bodies. The aim was to survey the relevant local units of each union or, in the case of ver.di, the three trade groups. In March 2015 (in case of ver.di in June), the unions sent out an electronic version of the questionnaire to each full-time official responsible for the relevant local unit, whereby care was taken to avoid overlaps. Respondents were asked to provide answers on behalf of the entire unit they were in charge of. We asked them to consider any relevant management activity since 2013. By January 2016, we had received 190 completed questionnaires. The response rates from local union units within the jurisdiction of IG BCE and IG Metall were 80 % and 66 % respectively. NGG could secure a response rate of 42 %. Unfortunately, ver.di could not encourage sufficient numbers of local union officials in the three trade groups to participate in the survey. The response rates in the three chosen trade groups ranged between 12.5 % and 13.8 %. This did not allow for a differentiated analysis by trade group.

In the following we will first report on the collated results of the examples of attempts by management to avoid the initial election of a works council as well as measures taken against works councils which had already been established. We will then analyse different company characteristics associated with those establishments which were identified as cases displaying employer resistance.

While 56 % of our respondents indicated hostile activity geared towards prohibiting or obstructing the election of a works council, a large minority (44 %) were not aware of any attempts. This does not necessarily indicate that in these cases there is no such activity; it simply means that no such activity has been brought to the attention of the union official concerned.

4.1 Obstructing the Election of Works Councils

Those respondents who reported activity listed 276 cases related to the same number of establishments in which management pursued activities against the election of a works council. In about a third of those cases (36 %), management succeeded with its strategy by virtue of the election of a works council not taking place.

Two of the unions participating in our survey (IG Metall and IG BCE) were also able to provide us with detailed data on the total number of works council bodies in those local union districts which had taken part in our survey. Data on the total number of works council elections was provided from the national union headquarters for the years 2013 to 2015. This was the same time frame in which anti-union behaviour on the part of employers was reported in our questionnaire. It was also identified whether a works council body was elected for the first time (indicating that this works council had been established anew) or had already existed prior to the election. In total, for those 138 local IG Metall and IG BCE districts that participated in our survey, 10 445 works council elections had been recorded between 2013 and 2015. Our respondents from those 138 local districts that participated in the survey identified 179 establishments where employers had tried to obstruct the election of a works council. This equates to about 1.7 % of all elections. If, however, we just focus on those 835 establishments (again, all cases in the 138 participating IG Metall and IG BCE districts only) where a works council had been elected for the first time the picture turns out to be much different: In 16.3 % of all cases where employees and their unions had tried to establish a works council, they were faced with resistance from the employer.

It should be noted that this is a very conservative estimate; to calculate this figure we excluded all those cases of employer anti-union behaviour where respondents identified that due to employer resistance the election of a works council had not been successful. This was necessary because cases of "obstructed elections" had not been recorded in the union statistics. In addition, we assume the system of election reporting by the union headquarters to be very formalised and routine-based while our written survey depends much more on the individual knowledge and exposure to the situation of our respondents. Following on from this, hostile behaviour by employers is potentially underestimated while we assume reporting on the total number of works council bodies (our denominator) to be more accurate.

Again, returning to the full dataset with all four union jurisdictions (see *table 3*), there are some differences when comparing the four union jurisdictions with each other.

TABLE 3

Knowledge of attempts to obstruct the establishment of a works council

	Attempts to obstruct election of a works council in % of all respondents (n = 190)	Average number of cases per district with a positive response (n = 107)
Ver.di[A]	68	2.6
NGG	76	2.6
IG Metall	53	2.6
IG BCE	43	2.3
All	56	2.6

A Three trade groups only (retail and wholesale, postal services, logistics and special services)

Source: Second WSI survey on management hostility towards works councils (2015)

The NGG stands out as the jurisdiction where attempts to obstruct the election of a works council occurred most frequently (76 % of responding local units reported at least one incident in comparison to 56 % of all unions). When focusing on the number of cases of obstruction per local unit (only those 107 units which reported any activity at all) union officials in the chemical and mining industries reported less activity than all the other unions. If there are any attempts to obstruct the election at all, on average there are 2.3 cases per local unit in the jurisdiction of the IG BCE, while this number is 2.6 for all unions included in our survey.

Further qualitative research will be needed to explore the reason for these discrepancies and also for the fact that if a unit reports incidence, it often reports more than one case. It is very likely that there is a strong relationship between union activity directed at establishing new works councils and management opposition. In other words: Those units which are not aware of any such opposition probably put less focus in their day-to-day work on the establishment of works councils than others. Feedback gathered from union officers at union meetings where we presented our data points in that direction.

We further asked respondents to indicate the kind of measures management had taken to avoid or obstruct the election of works councils. Because we restricted the possibility to give detailed information to a maximum of five establishments per unit, we were able to report detailed information for 239 of our 276 cases only.

Table 4 shows that the most widespread practice employed to obstruct the election of a works council is the intimidation of candidates. Particularly in small and medium-sized establishments, where social contact between owner, management and employees is more personal and direct, candidates can be quite perceptive of this tactic. The same might be true for employer tactics such as supporting business-friendly candidates (43 %) or offering benefits if certain candidates give up the plan to run for the works council election (19 %). In a majority of cases management pursues just between one and three of those tactics (listed in *table 4*, including the category "others") at any one

TABLE 4

Measures taken by management to obstruct works council elections

Measure taken by management	Frequency (in %)
Intimidation of works council candidates	72
Obstructing the creation of an election committee	68
Supporting pro-employers' candidates	43
Denying the union access to the establishment	20
Offering benefits if candidates give up plan to run for works council election	19
Firing works council candidates	18
Refusing to provide election documents (staffing lists)	16
Firing members of election committee	13
Targeted company restructuring	10
Plant closure, outsourcing, relocation of the entire establishment	2
Others	17

WSI Mitteilungen

Source: Second WSI survey on management hostility towards works councils (2015)

time. 29 % of establishments, however, use the wider range of the repertoire and employ four or more different tactics to prevent the establishment of a works council.

Also, as our respondents have indicated, about 75 % of those establishments for which activities against works council elections have been reported employ less than 200 persons. In addition, in 52.2 % of establishments where some activity geared against works councils had been reported, that establishment was an owner-operated business.

Obstructing the establishment of a works council usually starts rather early in the process. In 68 % of cases, management tried to prevent the election committee being set up; this is the elected legal body which organises and monitors the works council election. Even more robust measures were the dismissal of works council candidates (18 %) or of members of the election committee (13 %). All of these activities represent outright violations of the Works Constitution Act. In terms of the choice of specific tactics, however, employers might not resort to measures such as firing candidates or firing members of the election committee; tactics which could be more easily challenged in the courtroom. In order to be prosecuted, however, they must successfully be brought before the courts, an action workers and their union alike might shy away from as long as more subtle employer tactics are more difficult to prove in court.

In total, in only 16 of 239 establishments (6.7 %), for which detailed information on employer measures against the establishment has been made available, unions or employees filed for criminal charges in the labour court (87.4 % did not file a case while another 5.9 % did not know). As predicted, this share is above the average when respondents indicated that the employer had fired either candidates or members of the election committee or had initiated restructuring. In cases where a motion with the court had been filed, respondents had identified on average 5.0 different employer measures against the establishment of a works council, in cases where such a motion was not filed, this average amounted to only 2.8 different measures.

Frequently, employers who aim to avoid the election of a works council, seek external support. It is striking that 40 % of our respondents indicate that in pursuing their anti-works council strategy, management sought support from law firms or consultants. In 41 % of cases the respondent did not know the case well enough to give an assessment. Only 18 % of respondents were confident that a third party was not involved. In Germany, specialised law firms and legal consultants assisting employers to stay "union free" are less established than they are in, for example, the United States of America. Legal assistance is traditionally provided through employers' associations and their lawyers. In recent years, however, specialised attorneys and law firms who are prominently engaged in assisting employers to get rid of their works councils have gained more prominence (Esser/Schröder 2011, p. 46ff.). Our findings suggest that this new market for "works council avoidance" might be growing, for when excluding those "did not know" cases, our data reveals that the chances that four or more tactics are employed at a time increase by almost 20 percentage points when respondents indicate that a law firm or consultancy has been involved.

4.2 Measures Taken against Established Works Councils

Overall, management measures taken against established works councils with the aim of getting rid of the body, or prominent representatives, are less widespread than attempts to prevent the initial creation of such a worker representation body *(table 5)*.

Only 39 % of our responding local union units have reported attempts to either fire works council members, to dissolve the works council altogether or to force members

TABLE 5

Knowledge about management measures against existing works council

	Know about measures against existing works councils in % of all respondents (n = 190)	if yes, average number of cases by local unit (n = 69)
Ver.di [A]	54	1.5
NGG	48	1.7
IG Metall	33	1.8
IG BCE	38	1.5
All	39	1.7

A Three trade groups only (retail and wholesale, postal services, logistics and special services)

Source: Second WSI survey on management hostility towards works councils (2015)

of a works council to leave. Remembering that the share of units which have indicated any attempts to obstruct the creation of such an interest representation body is 56 %, it appears that once a works council has successfully been set up, management in general tend to come to an arrangement with the body or consider it too costly to attack.

If management engages in action against already existing works councils, the most frequent measure employed is forcing works council members to resign from their position (49 % of all cases). In a further 40 % of cases, works council members were dismissed and in 25 % of all cases an employer went to the court to try to dissolve an existing works council. According to section 23 of the Works Constitution Act, either an employer, a quarter of the workforce or a union can file a suit to dissolve a works council in case of gross misconduct. In 12 % of cases an employer endeavoured to remove a works council by way of splitting the establishment up into new separate entities. Finally, in 7 % of our cases the employer had even closed down the entire plant.

If we look at the number of reported incidents in relation to establishment size it is striking that reported anti-works council activity clearly peaks in establishments which employ between 50 and 200 employees (*figure 1*).

FIGURE 1

Incidents of obstruction of works council elections and action against elected works councils by size of establishment

Percentage shares of reported incidents

■ Obstruction of election

■ Action against elected works councils

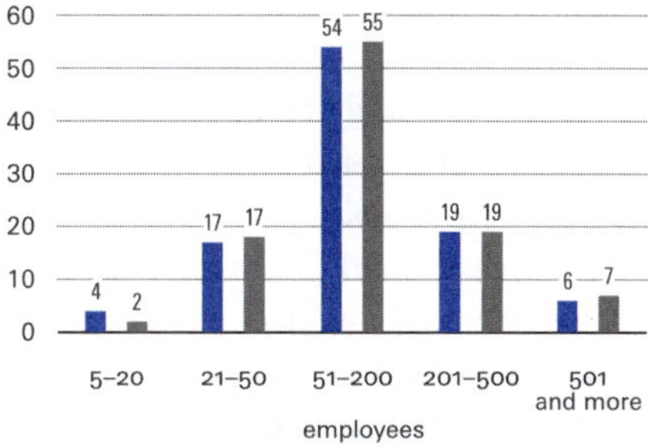

Source: Second WSI survey on management hostility towards works councils (2015)

WSI Mitteilungen

Since we have no empirical data about the total number of establishments in a given size band where workers or unions have ever considered or attempted to establish a works council, we cannot estimate the likelihood within a category of a certain size that obstructive measures occur. However, it is obvious that union officials report significantly less incidents of anti-works council activity in establishments with more than 500 employees. From what we know from unions, we assume that this circumstance is related to the fact that many of these works councils were created in the course of a reorganisation of parent companies – companies, in which unions and works councils had already been an established feature of labour relations. On the other side of the spectrum we assume that attempts to establish a works council in establishments with up to 20 employees are rare. Some of the reasons why unions are reluctant to get engaged here will be discussed below. We conclude from our data that if there are attempts to establish a works council, it is in the small and medium-sized establishments

TABLE 6

Share of owner-operated establishments with incidents of hostile practices

Percentage shares

	(a) Obstruction of establishment of works councils	(b) Measures against existing works councils	(c) Reference Group WSI works council survey 2015
Ver.di[A]	20	24	24
NGG	61	39	36
IG Metall	59	48	50
IG BCE	59	27	36
All	52	39	34

A Three trade groups only (retail and wholesale, postal services, logistics and special services)

Source: Second WSI survey on management hostility towards works councils (2015);
WSI works council survey 2015

that employees and unions meet employer resistance. Employer hostility towards works councils is also much more frequent when an establishment is owner-operated, as we can learn from *table 6*.

As a benchmark in column (c) of *table 6* we have first documented the share of owner-operated establishments within our general population. The calculations are based on the WSI works council survey which is a representative bi-annual survey of establishments with a works council. The survey excludes establishments without a works council, those within the public sector and establishments with less than 20 employees. In total, the 2015 survey drew 4125 valid responses. In order to be able to compare this data with our second WSI survey on management hostility, we have made another two adjustments: To calculate the share of ownership-run establishments we have included only those units which are within the jurisdiction of our four unions. Furthermore, to control a size bias we have also excluded those units with more than 500 employees. After having made those adjustments, the total share of establishments run by the owner is 34 %. When we now turn to those 100 establishments for which measures taken against existing works councils have been reported (column b) the share of ownership-controlled units is higher – at 39 %, five percentage points above the level indicated for the reference group.

Turning to those 239 cases where employers have sought to obstruct the election of a works council, the share of ownership-controlled establishments is even higher, increasing to 59 % of cases within the jurisdiction of IG Metall and even 61 % of cases observed by NGG.

This data indicates that works councils, as one of the key institutions of employment relations in Germany, fail to find broad acceptance within the group of employers who run their establishments on their own. In this part of the German economy, the paternalistic attitude of "nobody tells me how to run my business" still seems to be widespread. While earlier studies of the small firm sector (Kotthoff/Reindl 1990; Hilbert/Sperling 1993) have already described such a paternalistic attitude as being one important version of what Kotthoff calls a "plant-level social order", it is striking that ownership as a key attribute turns out to be a very powerful explanatory variable to help explaining the segmentation of co-determination in Germany. To follow up on the different patterns of diffusion of employer anti-works council practices, we now turn to analysing the effect of industry affiliation.

5 Union Activity and Union Avoidance

Employers cannot be expected to proactively encourage the establishment of a works council. As mentioned above an unknown but presumably substantial number of establishments without works councils have none because neither employees nor a union ever tried to establish one. We do not know why employees in particular in SMEs are reluctant to push for a works council. There are no representative surveys on this matter. It can be assumed that some employees will not be informed about the advantages of a workplace representation and others in particular in small workplaces for one reason or another might deem such an institution not necessary. But lack of knowledge or interest cannot fully explain the large number of non-works council establishments. However, from what we know from union experience and the literature, the fear of employees being negatively sanctioned if they challenge a hostile employer on the matter is certainly another reason (Bormann 2007; Huhn 2001). When employees decide to start the procedure to establish a works council they need commitment and courage. In particular, if it can be expected that there will be resistance from the employer they will require the support of the union in place.

Whether the union gets actively involved in the establishment of a works council depends on the circumstances. Especially in industries with very many small workplaces, as is the case in big retail chains with virtually thousands of outlets, the union will try to conclude a collective agreement to establish a works council structure whereby one body covers more than one outlet. However, the power of unions to push through such an agreement against an unwilling employer is limited as the union at this stage is usually in the beginning of an organising process which itself often depends on the establishment of works councils (Dribbusch 2003). In 2002 the big German drugstore chain DM, with at the time 11 000 employees, proposed to ver.di the negotiation of a collective agreement to establish works councils across all its outlets after ver.di had successfully helped to establish the first ever works council in the company in October 2001. The reason for this proposal being that the company wanted to avoid further conflicts (Dribbusch 2003, p. 146, fn. 6). Other big retailers, as for example the big discount chain Lidl, have so far successfully resisted such agreements (Hamann/Giese 2005; Turner 2009, p. 301f.).

Moving beyond the case of retail, and focusing on the responses we received from IG BCE and IG Metall, it is striking that they are almost split in half: into those districts which do not report one single incident of anti-works council activity and those which report at least one such incident (68 districts and 70 districts respectively). This particular diffusion of anti-works council activity within the union landscape deserves some further attention.

A first explanation might be the different number of establishments within the jurisdiction of different local union units. According to this, districts with a larger number of works councils could be expected to produce more cases of anti-works council conduct when compared with those districts with a smaller number of works council bodies. A closer look at the number of works councils, however, does not confirm that pattern as we have districts with about the same number of works councils which nevertheless differ fundamentally in their assessment. The share of newly elected bodies amongst all works councils is on average the same in both types of districts within the IG BCE sample (8 % each). It differs slightly within the whole IG Metall sample – 7 % newly elected bodies in districts with no reported incidents against 9 % in those which reported positively. While these statistics do not allow for a straightforward conclusion, the background talks we had with unionists when we presented our first findings in union seminars led us to the assumption that the number of reported incidents by a district might also be influenced by union activity. In other words, if a local union decides not to get involved in complicated or potentially conflictual cases, for example by largely abstaining from organising small workplaces, the chances of a hostile employer ever being challenged on the question of having a works council are limited. On the other hand, the likelihood of encountering employer resistance is significantly increased in those areas where local unions more frequently enter contested territory.

In 2017, in order to learn a little more about the motivation of local union districts to engage in the establishment of works councils, we approached two local districts of IG Metall to conduct two explorative semi-structured interviews. The first, referred to as district A, had not reported any instance of employer obstruction against the establishment of works councils while the second, district B, had reported an above average number of such incidents. Both districts covered a broadly similar number of establishments with a works council (120 and 115 respectively) but differed considerably in size and structure. District A is characterised by one major employer from the automotive industry. Two thirds of the employees covered by the 120 work councils in A are found in establishments with more than 500 employees. District B is much more characterised by SMEs. Almost 40 % of employees work here in establishments with up to 200 employees, another 40 % work in workplaces having 201 to 500 employees.

The IG Metall representative of A emphasised the special structure of the district and pointed in particular to the dominance of the larger establishments in terms of employment and therefore also in terms of potential members. While he was convinced that all establishments with at least 200 employees had a works council he admitted that there were new industrial locations with 100 to 150 employees which had still not been organised. Although the district reported no incidents of employer resistance to the establishment of works councils he said that in two establishments with a new works council the body was not respected by the employer. Greenfield organising was not considered to be an interesting option to increase overall membership levels in the district. It would be much more promising to increase union density in the big plants in the district where access to employees was already given. In fact, two thirds of the employed members of IG Metall in district A were found in the two handfuls of establishments with 1000 and more employees and only 14 % of active members worked in establishments with up to 200 employees.

In district B, which overall has half the size of district A, the situation was analysed in a completely different way. The full-time union official who was engaged in organising new workplaces and establishing new works councils emphasised that given the structure of the district she could not ignore the relevance of SMEs. About 60 % of IG Metall membership in district B is found in SMEs with up to 500 employees.

According to the officials there were some 40 to 60 small establishments with less than 100 employees within the district which had not yet been organised and were left without a works council. Unfortunately there were also cases of establishments with more than 100 or even 200 employees where nothing was moving forward because employees were afraid of getting involved in the union.

The local union made the decision to support an initiative towards the establishment of a works council based on a case by case examination. If the situation looked encouraging, even a 10 % density was considered to be a sufficient starting point. According to the union official, the approach considered to be the most promising in her experience was first to establish a works council then to push for bargaining coverage. It would mostly be in this second stage that employees would get organised. In the interview the official underlined what was already visible in the response to the survey that to her knowledge almost every effort to establish a new works council was met by some form of employer resistance. All in all, the official admitted that establishing a works council in adverse circumstances was a highly demanding affair for all those involved on the employee side but nevertheless the overall balance had been positive for the district. Membership development has improved over recent years and is amongst the top tier within the larger regional organisation of IG Metall.

As these two cases suggest – albeit based on a limited empirical basis – the diffusion of employers' activities against works councils does somewhat follow union activity which focuses on the creation of new works council bodies. The pro-active support of the creation of works councils by local unions – as our two cases indicate – is in part driven by the particular company structure and membership base within each local union unit.

6 Discussion and Conclusion

Although active opposition to the establishment of works councils and aggressive an-ti-works council strategies by employers are not the predominant features of German industrial relations, they are more than a marginal footnote. The full extent of anti-union strategies, however, remains very difficult to assess and is a challenge for future research. We see the tip of the iceberg but we cannot tell how much is hidden under water. There are indicators that there is antipathy amongst employers to get involved with a union especially in newly-established enterprises and in industries without tra-ditional union presence but only meaningful union activity or initiatives of employees to organise themselves reveal which employer is prepared to take anti-union action.

The data on works council coverage show that size is a crucial factor. In general it is more difficult for employers to prevent works councils in larger workplaces. This is strongly related to the fact that large workplaces are on average much more likely to have a union presence, not least because they have a greater potential for activists and attract more organising activity by unions (cf. for Germany Dribbusch 2003). So it does not come as a surprise that it is particularly in SMEs where we find evidence of union-avoidance activity. However, as can be seen in German retail, small workplaces may well be part of powerful business organisations that give the employer additional leverage. It also appears that single employers or family-run businesses are more likely to be engaged in union avoidance. Finally it seems that the tradition of workplace rela-tions at the establishment level, or in industry, is of importance. The more spectacular reports about active anti-unionism are usually related to businesses or industries with only weak forms of institutionalised industrial relations – or even none at all. So the tradition of industrial relations in a given industry matters too.

The forms of anti-unionism considered in this article are shaped by the industrial relations framework. Within the German system, the establishment of a works council is a hurdle which is seen to be of similar importance to union building as elsewhere the recognition agreement. Although the presence of a works council does not guarantee substantial membership, it is very rare to find significant membership in workplaces without a works council. It takes an effort to establish a works council and it involves risks and costs, precisely because unions or employees usually have to consider em-ployer opposition. The obstruction of works councils must therefore be considered as a means used by employers to keep the union off the premises. These strategies require more than just a declaration and it is not without good reason that specialised law firms offer employers their detailed services.

As Katz and Darbishire (2000) emphasised almost 20 years ago, different employ-ment-relations systems converge as they allow for the diversity of a limited range of competing labour relations patterns within one country. As our results indicate, how-ever, the patterns through which this diversity emerges are very complex; while we see powerful influences such as ownership, size, and industry at work, they do not submit to a simple core/periphery logic. As our analysis reveals, manufacturing is hardly a safe haven for the employee voice.

A very interesting aspect is the activity of the unions. There is strong indication that the differing extents of local union reporting on anti-works council activity carried out by employers is in part influenced by strategic choices made by unions in devoting personal and material resources to the organising of greenfield sites. Given the limits of resources unions have at their disposal and the necessity to stabilise membership levels, it is understandable that unions often opt to expand in those areas where they are already strong. However, given the changing structure of the economy, the ongoing shift of employment to the service sector and the increasing dominance of small and medium-sized workplaces, union will have to make hard choices if they do not wish to be relegated to shrinking niches of union strongholds.

REFERENCES

Behrens, M. / Dribbusch, H. (2014): Arbeitgebermaßnahmen gegen Betriebsräte: Angriffe auf die betriebliche Mitbestimmung, in: WSI-Mitteilungen 67 (2), pp. 140–148

Behrens, M. / Helfen, M. (2016): The organizational foundations of social partnership, in: British Journal of Industrial Relations 54 (2), pp. 334–357

Böhm, S. / Lücking, S. (2006): Orientierungsmuster des Managements in betriebsratslosen Betrieben. Zwischen Willkürherrschaft und Human Resource Management, in: Artus, I. / Böhm, S. / Lücking, S. / Trinczek, R. (eds.): Betriebe ohne Betriebsrat. Informelle Interessenvertretung in Unternehmen, Frankfurt a. M. / New York, pp. 107–139

Bormann, S. (2007): Angriff auf die Mitbestimmung. Unternehmensstrategien gegen Betriebsräte – der Fall Schlecker, Berlin

Doellgast, V. / Lillie, N. / Pulignano, V. (2018): Reconstructing solidarity. Labour unions, precarious work, and the politics of institutional change in Europe, Oxford

Dribbusch, H. (2003): Gewerkschaftliche Mitgliedergewinnung im Dienstleistungssektor. Ein Drei-Länder-Vergleich im Einzelhandel, Berlin

Ellguth, P. / Kohaut, S. (2018): Tarifbindung und betriebliche Interessenvertretung. Ergebnisse aus dem IAB Betriebspanel 2017, in: WSI-Mitteilungen 71 (4), pp. 299–306

Esser, C. / Schröder, A. (2011): Die Vollstrecker. Rausschmeißen, überwachen, manipulieren. Wer für Unternehmen Probleme löst, Munich

Greifenstein, R. / Kißler, L. / Lange, L. (2017): Trendreport Betriebsratswahlen 2014, Düsseldorf, online available at: https://www.boeckler.de/pdf/p_study_hbs_350.pdf [accessed 29 November 2018]

Hamann, A. / Giese, G. (2005): The Black Book on the Schwarz Retail Company Lidl. Selling cheap at the employees' expense, Berlin/Nyon

Hilbert, J. / Sperling, H.-J. (1993): Die kleine Fabrik. Beschäftigung, Technik und Arbeitsbeziehungen, Munich/Mering

Huhn, J. (2001): Die Schlecker-Kampagne 1994–1995. Gewerkschaften als soziale Bewegung, Mannheim

Katz, H. C. / Darbishire, O. (2000): Converging divergences. Worldwide changes in employment systems, Ithaca/London

Kempen, O. / Zachert, U. (eds.) (2006): TVG Tarifvertragsgesetz – Kommentar für die Praxis, 4th ed., Frankfurt a. M.

Köhnen, H. (2006): Unternehmenskultur und Personalpolitik. Zur Situation der Beschäftigten und der Interessenvertretung bei H & M, Hans-Böckler-Stiftung: Arbeitspapier (119), Düsseldorf

Kotthoff, H. / Reindl, J. (1990): Die soziale Welt kleiner Betriebe. Wirtschaften, Arbeiten und Leben im mittelständischen Industriebetrieb, Göttingen

Küppers, K. (2012): Die Schlecker-Saga, in: taz. die tageszeitung, March 24/25, 2012, pp. 16–18

Logan, J. (2006): The union avoidance industry in the United States, in: British Journal of Industrial Relations 44 (4), pp. 651–675

Müller-Jentsch, W. / Weitbrecht, H. (eds.) (2003): The changing contours of German industrial relations, Munich/Mering

Müller-Jentsch, W. (ed.) (1993): Konfliktpartnerschaft: Akteure und Institutionen der industriellen Beziehungen, 2nd ed., Munich/Mering

Streeck, W. (2016): Von Konflikt ohne Partnerschaft zu Partnerschaft ohne Konflikt: Industrielle Beziehungen in Deutschland, in: Industrielle Beziehungen 23 (1), pp. 47–60

Turner, L. (1998): Fighting for partnership. Labor and politics in unified Germany, Ithaca/London

Turner, L. (2009): Institutions and activism. Crisis and opportunity for a German labour movement in decline, in: Industrial & Labour Relations Review 62 (3), pp. 294–312

ver.di Bundeskongress (2015): 4. ver.di Bundeskongress, Leipzig, 2015: Tagesprotokoll 22. September

Wohland, U. (1995): Kampf um soziale Mindeststandards. 6 Monate Auseinandersetzung um die Drogeriekette Schlecker, in: Express. Zeitung für sozialistische Betriebs- und Gewerkschaftsarbeit (4), pp. 9–10

AUTHORS

MARTIN BEHRENS, PD Dr., is Senior Researcher at the Institute of Economic and Social Research (WSI) within the Hans-Böckler-Foundation in Düsseldorf, Germany. His field of research covers labour relations in national and comparative perspectives, including employers' associations, works councils and trade unions.

 E-Mail: Martin-Behrens@boeckler.de

HEINER DRIBBUSCH, Dr. rer. pol., is Senior Researcher at the Institute of Economic and Social Research (WSI) within the Hans-Böckler-Foundation in Düsseldorf, Germany. His field of research covers industrial relations with a special focus on trade unionism, collective bargaining and industrial conflicts.

 E-Mail: Heiner-Dribbusch@boeckler.de

The Composition of German Works Councils

Results from the WSI Works Council Survey

Works councils must not necessarily be a perfect reflection of their workforces, but nor should they be a distortion. Where the social and demographic gap between works councils and their workforces is too large, this can potentially inflict an even worse level of representation on groups that are already poorly represented. The article begins with a representative overview of the make-up of works councils in Germany during the term of office that ran from 2014 to 2018 in a degree of detail that has only become possible through the data collected by the WSI Works Council Survey. This allows an in-depth analysis both of the socio-demographic composition and organisational features of works councils and the extent to which these diverge from their workforces. In particular, it highlights a "representation gap" for employees on fixed-term contracts and for women. [1]

HELGE EMMLER, WOLFRAM BREHMER

1 Introduction

Previous research on works councils has tended to focus on their legal foundations, the identification of typical organisational patterns, and the outcomes of workplace co-determination (Kißler et al. 2011). One enduring concern has been establishing whether there are any differences in economic performance between firms with works councils and those without (Jirjahn 2010). Such approaches have often ignored the specific circumstances under which works councils operate, one significant aspect of which is their internal structure; that is, their social composition and which employee groups are represented by these bodies, and to what extent. Our starting assumption here is that a detailed appreciation of such internal structures would also improve our understanding of the outcomes of the activities of works councils. This article sets out to fill this research gap using data from the 2015 WSI Works Council Survey, supplemented by the 2018 WSI Works Council Survey. [2]

---

[1] This article is a translation and expanded version of our contribution „Die Zusammensetzung von Betriebsräten: Ergebnisse aus der WSI-Betriebsrätebefragung 2015", published 2016 in: WSI-Mitteilungen 69 (3), pp. 201–210.

As well as describing the structural features of works councils, this article will also compare these with the characteristics of the workforces at the establishments covered by the survey. This provides an indication of which employee groups are over-represented and which under-represented. In other words, which employees "take on this challenging task" (Tietel 2006, p. 319).[3]

The article is structured as follows: It begins with an outline of the state of research on the composition of works councils and the data drawn on in this paper (section 2). This is followed by an analysis of the sectoral incidence of works councils (section 3). Section 4 considers some of the specific features of works councils, such as the use of time off and the overall length of office holding. Section 5 compares the social characteristics of works council members and workforces, specifically their age, gender, form of employment and educational attainment, and identifies where these coincide or diverge. The main results are summarised in section 6.

2 The Data

2.1 Data Sources on the Composition of Works Councils

Although there are a number of sources of representative data on works councils in Germany, aside from the WSI Works Council Survey these either do not deal with the internal structures of these bodies (this applies, for example, to the IAB Establishment Panel) or do not enable their structural features to be compared with workforce characteristics (for example, as in the "Trend Report on Works Council Elections" *[Trendreport Betriebsratswahlen]* and the surveys conducted by the IW). The four relevant surveys are as follows:

– The IAB Establishment Panel[4] is an annual survey of 16 000 establishments across all branches and establishment sizes conducted annually for the Institute for Employment Research *(Institut für Arbeitsmarkt- und Berufsforschung, IAB)*, which is attached to the German national employment service, the Federal Employment Agency (BA) (Ellguth et al. 2014). This very large sample provides a robust basis on which to estimate the number of works councils and their distribution by branch and establishment size. However, the survey does not collect any additional information about works councils.

---

2   WSI (Wirtschafts- und Sozialwissenschaftliches Institut) is the Economic and Social Research Institute at the Hans-Böckler-Foundation, Düsseldorf.

3   This and other quotations translated from the original German.

4   Details of this survey in English can be found at its website https://www.iab.de/en/erhebungen/iab-betriebspanel.aspx

- The "Trendreport Betriebsratswahlen" analyses survey returns submitted by works councillors in almost 15 000 establishments where employees are organised by four of the largest German trade unions affiliated to the German Confederation of Trade Unions (DGB): these are IG Metall (metalworking, electrical and electronic industry), ver.di (private and public services), IG BCE (mining, chemicals and energy), and NGG (food, beverages and catering). This survey, the most recent report of which was published in 2014 (Greifenstein et al. 2014), collects data on the structures of works councils and allows a longitudinal comparison between the works council elections held in 2010 and those in 2014. Data is collected on the level of trade union membership of office holders, the proportion of women, the turnover of works councillors, age, and which electoral procedures are used.
- The German Economic Institute *(Institut der deutschen Wirtschaft, IW)*[5] in Cologne carries out its own surveys on the results of the most recent works council elections via the regional *(Land)* federations of its affiliated employer associations. The most recent survey provides data from 1600 companies, which the IW concedes is "not representative" (Stettes 2015, p. 4). The main results deal with workforce participation in the elections, the number of works council members with time off, the gender and age of works councillors, the level of union membership, and the length of time works council chairs hold office.
- The WSI Works Council Survey *(WSI-Betriebsrätebefragung)* is a survey of works councils in Germany that has been conducted several times since 1997. It is the main source of data for the present article. The aims and methods of the survey are set out in the section that follows and in more detail in Baumann (2015) and infas (2015).

2.2 The WSI Works Council Panel 2015–2018

The WSI has conducted surveys of works councils across all branches and regions in Germany since 1997 on the issue of workplace co-determination. Its aim is to identify workplace problems and solutions, report on new developments in the field of co-determination and produce representative data on relevant workplace developments. The survey collects data on the make-up both of works councils and workforces at the establishments in the sample, including information on the age of office holders, the proportion of women, the level of union membership, and also the number of works council members entitled to time off, their seniority, and how long the works council has existed for.

The 2015 Works Council Survey was conducted for the WSI by the infas Institut, Berlin, between 21 January and 30 April 2015, with questionnaires sent to 4125 works councils. The sample was a random one drawn from a population of all establishments

---

5   IW is associated with the national employers' association, the BDA, and other employer groups. See https://www.iwkoeln.de/en.html

with more than 20 socially-insured employees and a works council. The data in this article refers to this sample, which was drawn from an address list held by the establishment database of the Federal Employment Agency. Since this list does not include telephone numbers or information about whether these establishments have a works council or not, the WSI survey required further initial detailed research to ascertain this information. Of the works councils identified, 53.1% indicated that they were willing to participate in the survey, a high response rate for what is a very detailed survey. One person was asked to participate in the survey in each establishment, typically the chair of the works council. Surveys were conducted by phone using CATI. The 125 interviewers were specially trained for this survey and the questionnaires were trialled in 214 pre-survey test interviews. More complex questions were subjected to a qualitative cognitive pre-survey test.

The 2015 WSI Works Council Survey collected data on a larger number of works council characteristics than its predecessors. For example, data was collected for the first time on forms of employment, levels of educational attainment, and works council composition by age. The survey offers a very effective means of achieving an up-to-date and representative picture of the distribution of a large number of works council characteristics in Germany during the period between the 2014 and 2018 works council elections.

The 2015 WSI Works Council Survey also represented the initial survey for a works council panel that was surveyed four times between 2015 and 2018. The final wave consisted of 2288 individuals (infas 2018) and is used in this paper as a source of some additional data on specific issues.

3   Incidence of Works Councils

Works councils may be set up under the provisions of the Works Constitution Act *(Betriebsverfassungsgesetz)* should employees wish to do so. Whether this happens will depend on a number of preconditions being met at workplace level (Artus et al. 2016). Moreover, when setting up a works council, employees may have to contend with resistance from their employer (Behrens/Dribbusch 2013, 2014; see also Behrens/Dribbusch in this volume). Around 10% of all eligible establishments[6] in Germany have a works council. [7] Ellguth/Kohaut (2018, p. 303f.) note that this proportion has remained fairly

---

6   Under the Works Constitution Act, an eligible establishment is one with five or more employees.

7   The distribution of private-sector establishments with a works council by branch and by establishment size, but not cross-tabulated, can be found in the annual report of the IAB Establishment Panel, published in the WSI journal "WSI-Mitteilungen" (most recently Ellguth/Kohaut 2018).

stable in recent years, but that the number of employees represented by them has fallen (for an explanation of this development, see Ellguth/Trinczek 2016).

Table 1 sets out the sectoral incidence of establishments with a works council. The data is from the IAB Establishment Panel and covers establishments with 20 or more socially-insured employees. The presentation allows branch and size effects to be considered separately. Irrespective of the branch to which an establishment belongs, the likelihood of having a works council clearly increases with establishment size. And since there are many more small than large establishments in Germany, only 31% of establishments with 20 or more employees have a works council, although in establishments with 100 or more employees, works councils are more the norm than the exception.

There are marked differences between branches in terms of the incidence of works councils that are not solely attributable to the establishment size typical of each branch. For example, the low density of works councils in construction and business services is not due solely to establishment size, as large establishments in these branches (500+ employees) also have fewer works councils. The converse is the case in mining and the production industries (excluding construction), and in financial services and insurance, where works councils are common even in small establishments. These differences can

TABLE 1

Sectoral incidence of establishments with a works council, 2014

Percentage shares

Branch	Establishment size (number of employees in employment subject to social insurance)					
	20–49	50–99	100–199	200–499	500+	All
Mining; production industries	23.0	57.9	68.1	87.3	92.1	45.9
Investment goods	14.7	46.7	71.3	83.9	98.6	39.4
Construction	8.4	30.7	68.8	77.9	68.2	17.1
Commerce	16.5	43.8	52.3	66.1	97.7	26.8
Transport and storage; hospitality	11.1	42.2	49.7	83.6	93.3	22.8
Information and communication	15.5	38.7	77.5	72.6	91.9	32.6
Financial services and insurance	55.5	65.5	71.2	84.6	100.0	62.8
Business services	17.8	23.7	39.7	43.7	76.8	23.9
Privately provided public services[A]	20.9	48.8	56.8	79.5	87.9	37.6
Other	18.8	42.6	48.4	76.8	71.3	30.2
Total	**17.1**	**42.2**	**58.0**	**74.0**	**91.1**	**31.4**

A Table 1 does not cover the public sector, which has separate arrangements for workplace employee representation (Personalräte [staff councils]). The proportion of eligible public sector establishments in public administration with such staff councils is considerably higher than eligible private sector establishments with a works council (Brehmer 2016).

Source: tailored evaluation by the IAB based on the IAB Establishment Panel, 2014; calculations undertaken by Peter Ellguth, IAB

WSI Mitteilungen

be explained by branch-specific features. For instance, setting up a works council is more difficult in branches in which many employees work outside the physical confines of the establishment, as in construction or in business services. Whether an establishment is covered by collective bargaining might also play a role, together with how employees perceive co-determination, as shaped by their occupational status and what might be customary for that branch. Overall, works councils are more common in branches characterised by a high level of collective bargaining and long-standing traditions of trade unionism (Ellguth/Trinczek 2016).

Equally, the age of establishments, which varies considerably between branches, might also play a role. Many digital business service firms are of very recent origin, for example. Works councils are also likely to have been set up when employees have faced the prospect of a business restructuring or crisis (see Artus et al. 2016). And such events will have probably been encountered more frequently the longer an establishment has existed. There is, of course, also a wide range, from establishments having existed for 50 years or more, to those set up in the last five years, the majority of which, not entirely accidentally, were constituted in 2014, the year of the most recent works council elections (*figure 1*). Almost half the work councils in existence in 2015 were set up between 1991 and 2010. And more than a quarter of existing works councils originate from the period before 1980. Not surprisingly, most of these older works councils are in large establishments with more than 500 employees and with a high proportion of works councillors who have held office over a long period (40 % and above in their third or higher term of office).

FIGURE 1

Time of setting-up the works councils

Percentage shares

■ Western Germany
■ Eastern Germany

Source: WSI Works Council Survey 2015; own calculation

WSI Mitteilungen

4 Works Council Structures

Before looking at the social structure of works councils in section 5 and contrasting this with the social structure of the workforce as a whole at the sample establishments, we consider a number of specific aspects of works councils, such as the use of time-off provisions, the overall length of office of works councillors, and the age and gender of works council chairs. These are aspects that cannot be compared with workforce characteristics.

4.1 Use of Time off

Under the provisions of the Works Constitution Act, holding office as a works councillor is a lay position, unremunerated as such, and exercised alongside a member's usual employment duties. In order to ensure that works council members do not suffer any detriment, the law stipulates that they should be relieved from some of these employment duties (Däubler et al. 2002, p. 754). In addition to this "usual" relief, and depending on the size of the establishment, section 38 of the Works Councils Act provides for a minimum number of employees to be given full release from work in order to carry out representative duties. For example, in establishments with between 200 and 500 employees, at least one works council member should be given full time off, to be granted in consultation with the employer.[8] Additional time off for other works councillors can be agreed with the employer. In practice, such time-off rights are not always made use of once the thresholds set out in section 38 of the Act are reached (Backes-Gellner/Mohrenweiser 2010, p. 421). In all, every eleventh works council member surveyed (9.4 %) had full time off from work. Adding in those works councillors on part-time release yields a proportion of 17.7 % of works council members who were either wholly or partly released from work, around every sixth works councillor.

Figure 2 compares the average number of employees with time off, irrespective of establishment size, with the minimum number provided for under section 38 of the Works Constitution Act. This is presented as works council seats rather than any proportional values. As provided for by the statute, the larger the establishment, the greater the number of works councillors with time off. Not all works councils made full use of their statutory entitlement, however: 8 % of works councils did not, or only partly, avail themselves of their legal rights in this area. On the other hand, 7.4 % of works councils had more employees with time off than their legal entitlement. Considering only those establishments with 200 or more employees – that is, above the first threshold at which an entitlement to time off begins – these divergences between actual and statutory time-off provisions become more apparent. At these larger establishments, 23.4 % did not make full use of their entitlement; 67.5 % used exactly their entitlement; and 9.1 % had agreed greater time-off provisions (Baumann/Brehmer 2015).[9]

8　The amount of time available for full-time release can also be re-assigned to a larger number of members in the form of part-time release.

9　Figures for the use of the minimum time-off entitlement relate only to establishments without any part-time release, as this can be taken on a rotating basis and does not add up in every instance to the equivalent time taken as full-time release. This therefore means that the appropriate number is 3221 cases rather than 4125.

Time off for works councillors is available on a full-time or part-time basis, or "as required".[10] Works councils can determine how their overall time-off entitlement is allocated to members. Part-time release is an attractive option for works councillors as it allows for a degree of professionalisation of works council work without requiring works council members to give up their regular work entirely. The problem with such arrangements, however, is that it is often difficult to maintain a clear boundary between usual working time and time set aside for works council activity. Although works councillors with part release are legally entitled to be free from their professional duties for the time required (as with full time off), in practice this only applies to a minority of works councils. The 2018 WSI Works Council Survey collected data on whether works councillors with part release were in fact appropriately relieved from some of their employment duties. Only 45.1 % indicated that this was "wholly the case". The majority of works councillors entitled to part-time release indicated that they were either not fully relieved to the extent to which they were entitled (41.5 %) or "not relieved at all" (13.4 %).

FIGURE 2

Use of time off provisions by establishment size

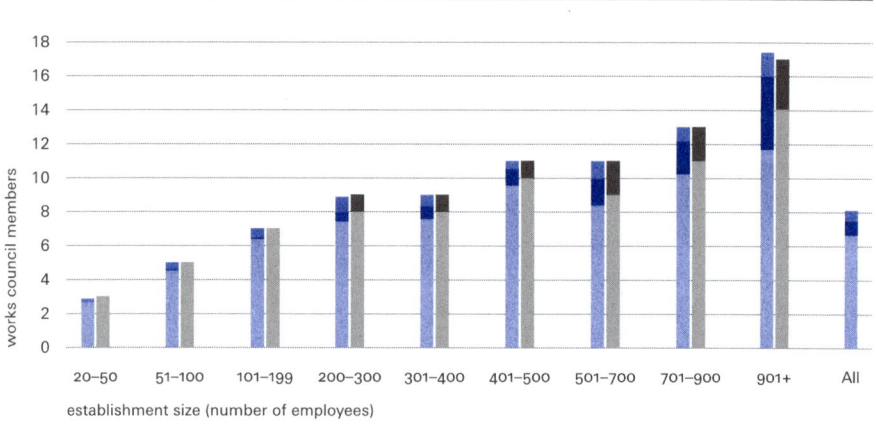

Absolute numbers

empirical observations   no release   full-time release   part-time release

legal entitlement   no release   release

Source: WSI Works Council Survey 2015; own calculation

---

10 Works councillors released "as required" are usually denoted as "not released". Employers must release such members from employment duties for any works council tasks, such as attending meetings. This depends on the requirement at the time and is not specified as a set proportion of their working hours.

4.2 Office Holding According to Overall Duration of Office

The survey collected data on how many members of each works cgouncil were in their first, second or more term of office; a term of office being four years. These three groups were fairly evenly distributed across all office-holders, with a slight bias towards those with greater seniority as works councillors: 34 % were in their first term of office, 30 % in their second, and 36 % in their third or more term of office. These figures differ only marginally from those of the "Trendreport Betriebsratswahlen" (35 %/24 %/41 %; Greifenstein et al. 2014, p. 12).

There is a clear size effect for terms of office. Large establishments have proportionally more works councillors with longer (uninterrupted) membership *(figure 3)*. In smaller establishments with fewer than 200 employees, there is a preponderance of shorter periods of office for individual works councillors. The ratio of shorter to longer periods of office is relatively balanced in establishments with up to 500 employees – with a slight tendency towards longer periods of office – but then with a much more pronounced shift to longer periods of office in establishments with more than 500 employees. There is a further increase in the proportion of works councillors in their third or more term of office in establishments with approximately 1750 employees and above. However, the number of such cases in our sample is very small. Nevertheless, in establishments with 900 employees or above, for which there were more cases, it was possible to be confident from the survey that a solid 50 % or more of works council members were in their third or more term or office, with just some 25 % in their first term of office.

4.3 Turnover of Works Council Members

Works councillors interviewed in 2015 were re-interviewed three years later to gauge the rate of turnover during the term of office that ran from 2014 to 2018. Only 26 % of works councils experienced no turnover in this period. For 36.8 %, at least one member left on age grounds, and for 60.5 % at least one member for other reasons. Between 2014 and 2018, 8.1 % of all works councillors in the survey left on age grounds and 19.1 % for other reasons.

4.4 Works Council Chairs

Those chairing works councils tend to be male and, on average, exactly 50 years old, with no difference between male and female chairs. In terms of age, works council chairs are concentrated in a fairly narrow band (see *figure 4*). More than a quarter are between 51 and 55, with around a half between 51 and 60. Only one in five is younger than 46.

Only one in four works councils is chaired by a woman (26.9 %). This corresponds with the figure of 29.1 % from the "Trendreport Betriebsrätewahlen" (ibid., p. 18). Female works council chairs are even less common where the works council as a whole is predominantly female: as *figure 5* indicates, women account for only 45 % of works

FIGURE 3

Duration of works council office by establishment size^A

Percentage shares

— works councillors in their first term of office

— works councillors in their third or more term of office

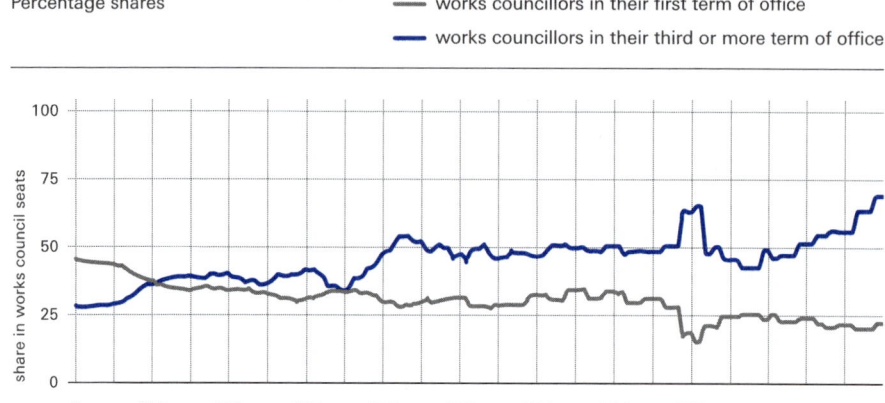

A   This is a kernel density estimate. On non-parametric regression methods, see, for example, Rohwer/Pötter 2001, chapter 8

Source: WSI Works Council Survey 2015; own calculation

council chairs even where between 60 and 70 % of seats are held by women. Moreover, in order for a works council to be predominantly female, there needs to be a very clear female majority in the establishment's workforce (see section 5.3). This suggests that the under-representation of women is cumulative; that is, where women are disadvantaged in terms of their representation on works councils as well as in the choice of chair, these two processes will reinforce each other.

5   Workforce and Works Council Characteristics

The following section compares the social and demographic make-up of workforces and works councils. After some initial thoughts as to whether a high level of structural equivalence between works councils and workforces is necessarily desirable, we consider the following characteristics: age, gender, education, form of employment, trade union membership and whether or not employees have a migration background.

FIGURE 5

FIGURE 4

Age groups of works council chairs

Percentage shares

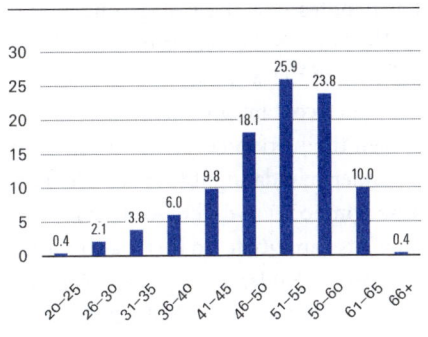

FIGURE 5

Share in female works council chairs by share in female works council members

Percentage shares

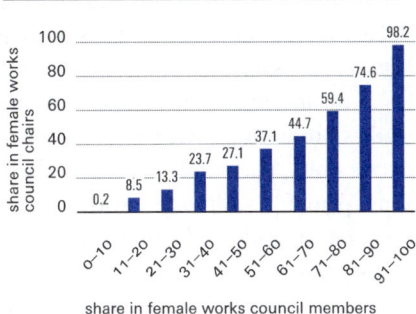

share in female works council members

Source: WSI Works Council
Survey 2015; own calculation

WSI Mitteilungen

Source: WSI Works Council
Survey 2015; own calculation

WSI Mitteilungen

5.1 Comparing the Social Characteristics of Works Councils and the Workforce

While collecting data on the social characteristics and make-up of works councils might be said to be a fairly uncommon exercise, comparing such data with the characteristics of the workforce is a rarity. Behrens (2009) used data from the survey "Arbeitnehmer-Meinungs-Monitor 2008"[11] to compare occupational biographies, the views of works councillors and other employees. Greifenstein/Kißler (2014) drew on three case studies and compared trade union membership, age and gender of works council members and their workforces, amongst other variables.

The present article builds on these studies and attempts to extend what we know about the over- and under-representation of certain employee groups. This is a descriptive exercise and no attempt is made to propose or test a hypothesis or offer an explanation as to why works councils have the composition they have – that is, whether and why individuals from certain employee groups either put themselves forward as candidates for office or are less likely to be elected – or the consequences of any particular social composition. This would include, for example, whether a high degree of coinci-

---

11   This was a representative telephone survey of roughly 2000 individuals for the Hans-Böck-ler-Foundation.

dence between the characteristics of works councils and their corresponding workforce is "desirable" in terms of leading to more effective representation.

Nevertheless, at this juncture some consideration of the main arguments involved is appropriate. Can a works council that diverges socially from its corresponding workforce – its electorate – be an effective representative? Greifenstein/Kißler (2014) argue that representativeness has two distinct dimensions: a "workplace-political" dimension and a "socio-structural" dimension. The former denotes how the works council conducts itself, for example vis-à-vis management. The latter is the degree of coincidence between the make-up of the works council and that of the workforce. These authors begin by noting that the Works Constitution Act does contain provisions that can be read as promoting a degree of equivalence between the workforce and their representatives (ibid., pp. 7 and 128) and in the case of gender mandating it (see also Behrens 2009, p. 304f.).[12] Although works councils whose composition differs from that of its electorate might be able to represent it "politically", its capacity to do this is also rooted "in the quality of its social representation" (Greifenstein/Kißler 2014, p. 126). Nonetheless, works councils with councillors having a generally higher level of education or vocational qualification can exercise a type of "political piloting" (ibid., p. 127). Schnabel (2008, p. 160) argues that a higher level of educational attainment can be conductive to "a constructive and informative role at the workplace, that is it promotes allocative [efficiency]". However, as Greifenstein/Kißler (2014, p. 127) note, the workforce would still need to understand and subscribe to the approach of a works council that was dominated by office-holders with higher levels of educational attainment.

Behrens (2009, p. 304) cites several arguments in favour of a high degree of coincidence between the social composition of works councils and their workforce; for example, the capacity to come to a shared view of problems, lower likelihood of corruptibility through having common interests, and higher legitimacy through greater social proximity. By contrast, "mobilising the maximum possible representative competence" (ibid.) might make such an identity undesirable. And if even there were a high degree of structural equivalence, this would not of itself guarantee that the interests of workforces and works councils would coincide given that interests are determined contextually and these two groups might on occasions occupy differing contexts (ibid., p. 305). One further argument advanced by Frick (2008) against a high degree of correspondence between representatives and represented, albeit "not entirely seriously", is the situation of the German Lower House of Parliament, the *Bundestag*, where no such identity prevails. "And should this be a reason to doubt the legitimacy of members of parliament and/or works councillors?" (ibid., p. 174).

---

12 The relevant section of the Works Constitution Act is as follows: Section 15 (1) states that "The works council should be composed as far as possible of employees of the various organisation units and the different employment categories of the workers employed in the establishment." On gender, see section 5.2 below.

Overall, there are plausible arguments for a high degree of coincidence of social charac-teristics between works councils and their electorate workforces, without this needing to consist in a one-to-one relationship. To quote Greifenstein/Kißler (2014, p.7): "The social profile of a works council does not have to be a direct reflection of the workforce, but nor should it be a distortion."

5.2 Workforces and Works Councillors According to Age and Gender

The WSI Works Council Survey classified works council office holders and workforces according to age into three main groups: younger than 30, between 30 and 55, and over 55. More than two-thirds of all works council members (68.9 %) were in the interme-diate group. This is perhaps not surprising as this spans a broad range and also repre-sents the majority of employees. However, given that this group accounts for just 53.3 % of all employees in establishments with a works council, this constitutes an evidently disproportionate over-representation on works councils. The overall proportion of em-ployees and works council members in the oldest group is almost the same (20.1 % and 20 %). This is at the "expense" of younger employees, whose presence on works councils (11.3 %) is much lower than their share of workforces (25.4 %). This is also indicated by the relatively extended periods of office and, on average, higher age of works council chairs. These results broadly coincide with those of Behrens (2009, p.323) who found that works councillors "were several years older" than the rest of the workforce. The proportion of works council members who were younger than 30 in the WSI Works Council Survey was only marginally higher than the value in the IW survey (11.3 % com-pared with 8.5 %) (Stettes 2015, p.13) and also the data from the "Trendreport Betriebs-rätewahlen" (where the proportion was 7.9 %) (Greifenstein et al. 2014, p.13). Greifen-stein/Kißler (2014, p.126) also had the impression that younger employees "were not sufficiently represented on works councils".

A number of factors might explain this under-representation. To begin, employees under 25 years of age are entitled to seek election to the specific workplace represen-tative forum for young people, known as JAV *(Jugend- und Auszubildendenvertretung)*. This does not overlap with the works council. In any event, it would be reasonable to assume that younger employees feel less affiliation with "their" workplace than more long-standing staff. The fact that younger employees are often on fixed-term contracts might also play a role (see section 5.3).

At 38.6 %, women account for a smaller proportion of works councillors than men. Women's share of seats is below 40 % in more than half of all works councils (53.9 %). Overall, women accounted for 42.4 % of employees in the establishments in our sample. In many establishments, women are clearly not represented on works councils in pro-portion to their share of the workforce. *Figure 6* contrasts the share of women in the workforce (x-axis) with the share of works council seats (y-axis). The jagged black line describes the share of women on the works council in relation to their share in the workforce. The blue line is purely theoretical and serves as a comparative measure; it represents the ideal-typical case of an exact correspondence between the share of women in the workforce and on the corresponding works council. For example, where 60 % of the workforce are women, 60 % of works councillors would also be women. This is evidently not the case. In some cases, there is a moderate over-representation of women on works councils in establishments in which women represent below 20 % of the workforce. Women's representation on works councils broadly keeps step where they account for 20 to 50 % of the workforce. This is possibly attributable to the requirements of section 15 (2) of the Works Constitution Act that protects groups that are in a minority in the workforce: "The gender that accounts for a minority of staff shall at least be represented according to its relative numerical strength whenever the works council consists of three or more". Once the share of women exceeds 50 %, however, they no longer benefit from this provision and are almost universally under-represented where this is the case. There is a detailed discussion of this issue in Baumann et al. (2017).

FIGURE 6

Proportion of women in workforces and works councils

Percentage shares   ▬ ideal-typical: one-to-one ratio

▬ empirical: share in works council seats by share in the workforce

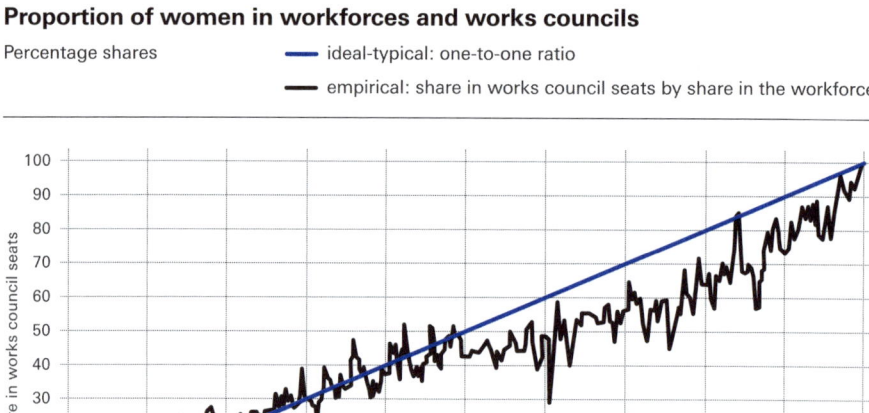

Source: WSI Works Council Survey 2015; own calculation

5.3 Works Council Membership According to Type of Employment

In recent years, atypical forms of employment have expanded in Germany and now account for some 40 % of all jobs (Keller/Seifert 2013). These changes in the structure of employment have been only partly reflected in the composition of workplace representative bodies. In particular, employees on fixed-term contracts rarely hold office as works councillors. While 9.9 % of all employees in establishments with a works council are employed on fixed-term contracts, less than 1 % (in fact 0.9 %) of works council seats are occupied by such staff. The situation is somewhat different for part-time workers, although the same broad trend can be identified: While some one in five employees in establishments with a works council are part-time workers (20.3 %), they account for just 14 % of works council seats.

Employees on fixed-term contracts accounted for only a small proportion of all employees in our sample. However, it is worth looking in more detail at those few establishments that had a high proportion of such employees. As *figure 7* shows, the proportion of works council seats held by employees on fixed-term contracts remains constant at around 1 %, whereby the share of these employees in the overall workforce of an establishment is below 40 %. Once the proportion of fixed-term employees exceeds this threshold, their representation on works councils grows several-fold. This suggests that a "critical mass" of fixed-term contracts at a workplace is needed to ensure that these employees are represented in workplace representative institutions.

That employees on fixed-term contracts are the most under-represented group of employees on works councils can be explained by some fairly familiar factors. On average, they are not employed for long and the duration of their employment contract is often shorter than the four-year term of office of a works councillor. Taking on the responsibility for workplace colleagues, and for the success of the establishment itself, usually grows out of a sense of affiliation with a place of work and colleagues. Developing this situation typically requires a longer period of employment, feeling accepted as a member of the core workforce, and viewing a job as a central part of one's future. Employees on fixed-term contracts also have to keep one eye on how and when their contract will end, especially as the expiry date draws near. Seeking office as a works councillor could spell the end of any hopes of moving on to an unlimited contract or having an existing arrangement renewed.

Both women and part-time workers are evidently under-represented on work

FIGURE 7

Employees on fixed-term contracts: share in works council seats by share in the workforce

Percentage shares

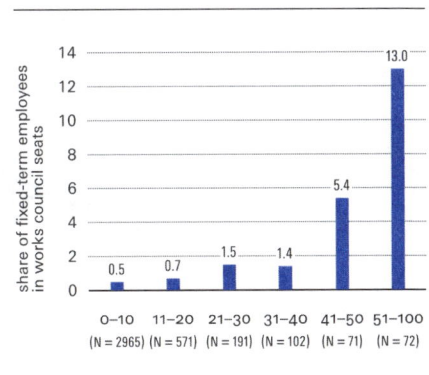

share of fixed-term employees in the workforce

Source: WSI Works Council Survey 2015; own calculation

WSI Mitteilungen

councils. And since women are much more likely to work part-time than men, these two overlapping groups can be considered together. Part-time work can prove a barrier to participating as a works councillor as it often coincides with the private obligations of employees, which often take up time that cannot easily be reduced and, moreover, co-exist with workplace obligations that are also not readily curtailed, especially where working hours are already shortened. Whether part-time employees who stand for election to works councils are elected less frequently via direct election than full-timers must remain, for now, a matter for speculation. And whether men put themselves forward more frequently for office, irrespective of whether they work full- or part-time, is also not known.

5.4 Educational Attainment

Data on the educational attainment of employees was broken down into three classes: those with a tertiary qualification, those with completed formal vocational training (but not a tertiary qualification), and unskilled and semi-skilled employees. However, the 2015 Works Council Survey collected data for works council members only on the issue of tertiary qualifications. In order to compare the educational attainment of works

FIGURE 8

Tertiary qualifications: workforce and works councils

Percentage shares ⸻ ideal-typical: one-to-one ratio

⸻ empirical: share in works council seats by share in the workforce

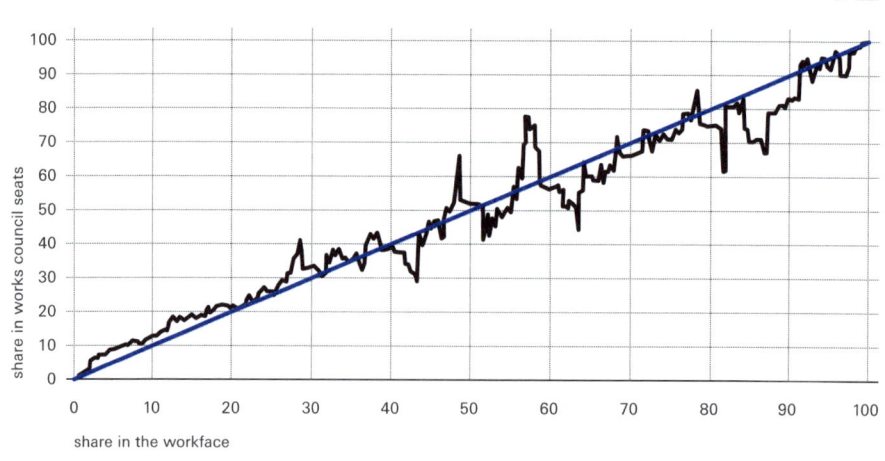

Source: WSI Works Council Survey 2015; own calculation

WSI Mitteilungen

councillors and workforces, *figure 8* contrasts the proportion of those with tertiary qualifications for works council members and employees. Overall, the proportion of works councillors with a tertiary qualification, at 19.9 %, is slightly higher than for the workforce as a whole, which stands at 17.9 %. In broad terms, they are essentially the same. In this respect, we have not been able to replicate Schnabel's finding (2008, p. 160) that works councillors tend to have lower levels of educational attainment than the general workforce. In fact, our results coincide more with those of Behrens (2009, p. 324) who also found only minor differences between works council members and employees. If anything, our results tend to suggest the opposite: that "the role of works councillor has become increasingly attractive for the skilled and highly educated" (Kotthoff 2008, p. 182).

5.5 Trade Union Membership

Works councillors are more inclined to be trade union members than other employees. This is not a new finding and confirms the data from previous research (Fitzenberger et al. 2006; Goerke/Pannenberg 2007; Behrens 2009). According to the WSI Works Council Survey, 62.1 % of all works council members were union members compared with 27.9 % of all employees in establishments with a works council. These values are well below those found by Greifenstein et al. (2014, p. 8) but are consistent with both the IW Survey (63.8 %) (Stettes 2015, p. 16) and with the "Arbeitnehmer-Meinungs-Monitor 2008" (63 %) (Behrens 2009, p. 310). Not all union members are in a union affiliated to the Confederation DGB, however. In all, 52.2 % of works councillors were members of DGB trade unions, around five out of six of those who were union members.

The level of trade union membership amongst works councillors differs according to the trade union (see *figure 9*). In the case of two trade unions, the Education and Science Workers' Union GEW *(Gewerkschaft Erziehung und Wissenschaft)* and the Railway and Transport Union EVG *(Eisenbahn- und Verkehrsgewerkschaft),* the number of cases in our

FIGURE 9

Level of union membership of workforces and works councillors in selected unions

Percentage shares

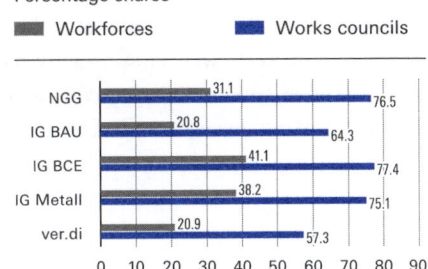

NGG: Gewerkschaft Nahrung-Genuss-Gaststätten (food, beverages and catering)
IG BAU: Industriegewerkschaft Bauen-Agrar-Umwelt (construction, agriculture and environment)
IG BCE: Industriegewerkschaft Bergbau, Chemie, Energie (mining, chemicals and energy)
IG Metall: Industriegewerkschaft Metall (metalworking, electrical and electronic industry)
ver.di: Vereinte Dienstleistungsgewerkschaft (private and public services)

Source: WSI Works Council Survey 2015; own calculation

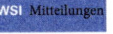

sample was too small to allow for a reliable estimate; and the Police Trade Union GdP *(Gewerkschaft der Polizei)* was not included in our sample which was based on the private sector. The overall percentage figures for works council members include membership in any trade union, not just a DGB affiliate.[13]

A comparison of the union density of workforces and works councillors in 2015 and 2018 indicates a slight decline for both, with a drop of 2.4 percentage points for workforces and 3.1 percentage points for works councillors. This might be attributable to the fact that non-union employees had moved onto works councils during this period as unionised members withdrew for various reasons. It could also be due to the fact that it was not possible to survey all works councillors prior to the 2018 works council elections. Larger and more highly-unionised workplaces might have been contacted later during the survey period and were not included in this comparison.

5.6 Works Council Membership for Employees with a Migration Background

"Migration background" is a concept that is difficult to define. In order to achieve some comparability with other studies, the best option would have been to draw on the definition used by the German Federal Statistical Office *(Statistisches Bundesamt).*[14] This is unsuitable for inclusion in a survey questionnaire, however, especially for a telephone interview. The WSI Works Council Survey therefore adopted a simplified definition that proved to be both usable, having been subject to cognitive pretesting with ten works councillors, but was also sufficiently specific; this states that employees with a migration background are "those born abroad or whose parents were born abroad". Based on this definition, the proportion of employees with a migration background as a percentage of all employees in establishments with a works council stood at 17.2 %; their share of works council seats was 8.6 %, exactly half. In relative terms, employees with such a background are under-represented in a ratio of 1 : 2. This is more favourable than being a fixed-term employee (1 : 10) but poorer than for women (approx. 1 : 1.1).

---

13 In figure 9, companies in which more than one trade union is represented are nevertheless assigned to only one trade union area of organisation. The allocation is made according to the union with the most members in the company. However, all union members, regardless of union, are counted for the purpose of calculating the degree of organisation per category.

14 The group "with a migration background consists of all persons who have migrated to the territory of today's Federal Republic of Germany after 1949, and of all foreigners born in Germany and all persons born in Germany who have at least one parent who migrated to the country or was born as a foreigner in Germany" (Statistisches Bundesamt 2014, p. 6).

6 Summary

This article has drawn on the 2015 WSI Works Council Survey to set out the main social and demographic characteristics of works council members and, where possible, compare these with those of the wider working population. This has shown that although works councillors do not represent a "Disneyland version" (Greifenstein/Kißler 2014, p. 125) of their corresponding workforces, they also do not represent a distortion. In broad terms, the scale of the characteristics in the WSI survey match those of other representative surveys, albeit with a level of union membership of works councillors that is considerably below that claimed in the "Trendreport Betriebsrätewahlen", a difference probably attributable to the nature of the latter study's sample. While works councillors are almost a mirror image of their workforces in terms of educational attainment, employees with other characteristics are under-represented. This applies especially to women (roughly 1 : 1.1), to employees with a migration background (1 : 2) and first and foremost to employees on fixed-term contracts (1 : 10).

These findings suggest that future surveys should attempt to gather data that might capture some of the complexities. For example, it would be worth exploring whether the under-representation of women is mainly a function of the fact that they tend to have a higher incidence of part-time work, and are less likely to seek office as a works councillor for this reason. Whether the under-representation of other groups is a function of the fact that they do not stand for office or whether they stand but are not elected should also be explored. Finally, some attention and analysis needs to be directed at the effects of under-representation for these groups.

REFERENCES

Artus, I. / Kraetsch, C. / Röbenack, S. (2016): Betriebsratsgründungen. Typische Phasen, Varianten und Probleme, in: WSI-Mitteilungen 69 (3), pp. 183–191

Backes-Gellner, U. / Mohrenweiser, J. (2010): Die Wirkung des Betriebsverfassungsgesetzes am Beispiel der Freistellung von Betriebsräten – ein Beitrag zur Rechtstatsachenforschung, in: Jahrbücher für Nationalökonomie und Statistik 230 (4), pp. 420–435

Baumann, H. (2015): Die WSI-Betriebsrätebefragung 2015, in: WSI-Mitteilungen 68 (8), pp. 630–638

Baumann, H. / Brehmer, W. (2015): Freistellungen: Nicht alle Betriebsräte schöpfen ihr Recht (voll) aus, http://www.mitbestimmung.de/html/freistellungen-nicht-alle-betriebsrate-1434.html (accessed 28 January 2016)

Baumann, H. / Brehmer, W. / Hobler, D. / Klenner, C. / Pfahl, S. (2017): Frauen und Männer in Betriebsräten: Zur Umsetzung des Minderheitenschutzes bei Betriebsratswahlen, Wirtschafts- und Sozialwissenschaftliches Institut: WSI-Report (34), Düsseldorf

Behrens, M. (2009): Unterscheiden sich Mitglieder von Betriebs- und Personalräten vom Rest der Belegschaften?, in: Industrielle Beziehungen 16 (4), pp. 303–326

Behrens, M. / Dribbusch, H. (2013): Anti-unionism in a coordinated market economy: the case of Germany, in: Gregor G. / Dundon, T. (eds.): Global Anti-unionism. Nature, Dynamics, Trajectories and Outcomes, Houndmills, pp. 83–103

Behrens, M. / Dribbusch, H. (2014): Arbeitgebermaßnahmen gegen Betriebsräte: Angriffe auf die betriebliche Mitbestimmung, in: WSI-Mitteilungen 67 (2), pp. 140–149

Brehmer, W. (2016): Mitbestimmung im öffentlichen Dienst – eine empirische Analyse der Determinanten vertiefter Personalratsbeteiligung, doctoral thesis, Universität Konstanz

Däubler, W. / Kittner, M. / Klebe, T. (2002): Betriebsverfassungsgesetz mit Wahlordnung. Kommentar für die Praxis, 8th, revised and updated ed., Frankfurt a. M.

Ellguth, P. / Kohaut, S. (2018): Tarifbindung und betriebliche Interessenvertretung. Ergebnisse aus dem IAB-Betriebspanel 2017, in: WSI-Mitteilungen 71 (4), pp. 299–306

Ellguth, P. / Trinczek, R. (2016): Erosion der betrieblichen Mitbestimmung – welche Rolle spielt der Strukturwandel?, in: WSI-Mitteilungen 69 (3), pp. 172–82

Ellguth, P. / Kohaut, S. / Möller, I. (2014): The IAB Establishment Panel – Methodological Essentials and Data Quality, in: Journal for Labour Market Research 47 (1), pp. 27–41

Fitzenberger, B. / Kohn, K. / Wang, Q. (2006): The Erosion of Union Membership in Germany: Determinants, Densities, Decompositions, Institute of Labor Economics: IZA Discussion Paper (2193), Bonn

Frick, B. (2008): Betriebliche Mitbestimmung unter Rechtfertigungsdruck. Die relative Bedeutung von Produktivitäts- und Umverteilungseffekten, in: Industrielle Beziehungen 15 (2), pp. 164–177

Goerke, L. / Pannenberg, M. (2007): Trade Union Membership and Works Councils in West Germany, in: Industrielle Beziehungen 14 (2), pp. 154–175

Greifenstein, R. / Kißler, L. (2014): Wen Betriebsräte repräsentieren. Sozialprofil von Interessenvertretungen und Belegschaftsstrukturen: Spiegelbild oder Zerrbild?, Berlin

Greifenstein, R. / Kißler, L. / Lange, H. (2014): Trendreport Betriebsrätewahlen 2014. Zwischenbericht, Hans-Böckler-Stiftung, Düsseldorf

IAB (Institut für Arbeitsmarkt- und Berufsforschung) (2015): Anteile der Betriebe mit Betriebsrat 2014. Sonderauswertung, unpublished manucsript

infas (Institut für angewandte Sozialforschung) (ed.) (2015): Methodenbericht WSI-Betriebsrätebefragung 2015, Bonn

infas (ed.) (2018): Methodenbericht WSI-Betriebsrätebefragung 2018, Bonn

Jirjahn, U. (2010): Ökonomische Wirkung der Mitbestimmung in Deutschland: ein Update, Düsseldorf

Keller, B. / Seifert, H. (2013): Atypische Beschäftigung zwischen Prekarität und Normalität, Berlin

Kißler, L. / Greifenstein, R. / Schneider, K. (2011): Die Mitbestimmung in der Bundesrepublik Deutschland. Eine Einführung, Wiesbaden

Kotthoff, H. (2008): Betriebsrat: ein Sammelbecken für Zukurzgekommene?, in: Industrielle Beziehungen 15 (2), pp. 178–184

Rohwer, G. / Pötter, U. (2001): Grundzüge der sozialwissenschaftlichen Statistik, Weinheim/Munich

Schnabel, H. (2008): Zur Diskussion über die betriebliche Mitbestimmung, in: Industrielle Beziehungen 15 (2), pp. 152–163

Statistisches Bundesamt (2014): Bevölkerung und Erwerbstätigkeit. Bevölkerung mit Migrationshintergrund, Ergebnisse des Mikrozensus, Fachserie 1, Reihe 2.2, Wiesbaden

Stettes, O. (2015): Betriebsratswahlen 2014. Ein Rückblick auf Basis der Betriebsratswahlbefragung, in: IW-Trends 42 (1), pp. 1–20

Tietel, E. (2006): Konfrontation – Kooperation – Solidarität. Betriebsräte in der sozialen und emotionalen Zwickmühle. Berlin

AUTHORS

HELGE EMMLER, Dr., is data manager at the Wirtschafts- und Sozialwissenschaftliches Institut (WSI) at the Hans-Böckler-Foundation. His main interests are research into works councils, theories of social research methods and data science.

@ E-Mail: helge-emmler@boeckler.de

WOLFRAM BREHMER, Dr., is a researcher at the WSI. His main research interests are works and staff councils.

@ E-Mail: wolfram-brehmer@boeckler.de

Trade Union Membership Policy: the Key to Stronger Social Partnership

The organising power of trade unions is the key to the future of social partnership. However, for several decades the organising power of German trade unions has been characterised by an eroding membership base, a fragmented membership structure and an enforcement crisis in collective bargaining policy. The article analyses the membership development in the unions of the German Trade Union Confederation (DGB) and argues for a strategic approach to membership policy.[1]

ANKE HASSEL, WOLFGANG SCHROEDER

1 Challenges for Trade Unions Today

The post-war consensus between employers, state and trade unions not only accompanied the economic revival of Germany after the Second World War, but efficient social partnership was a fundamental pillar of the social market economy. Although this consensus has not been completely rejected in Germany in the past two decades, its influence and creative power has clearly weakened. Sometimes this form of organised social partnership gives the impression that it has been reduced to the hub of the export-oriented industry. The regulatory concept of social partnership as a tool to balance different forces in the labour market seems to be increasingly less effective when taking into account the German economy as a whole. On the one hand, the service economy is more important than ever for employment, but unionisation and collective bargaining are especially weak. On the other hand, more and more employers are withdrawing from the system of binding agreements in the context of collective bargaining autonomy and social partnership.

---

1   This article is a translation of our contribution „Gewerkschaftliche Mitgliederpolitik: Schlüssel für eine starke Sozialpartnerschaft", published 2018 in: WSI-Mitteilungen 71 (6), pp. 485–496.

These issues raise questions for the trade unions about the basis on which they can position themselves, and with which goals and resources, in order to be able to represent the interests of the employees of the future, even under changed conditions. They need to improve their own attractiveness among employees in order to be able to claim a reliable influence over employers and actors in the political system. In this article, we first examine the deficits and problems of employee representation in the workplace and second, the organisational measures already taken by trade unions, as well as those that they intend to take, and new forms of reference relating to the needs and interests of the employees. Are the current needs and interests of employees adequately addressed through changes in organisational initiatives? What is the underlying logic of those changes, and what are the key features of the new union structure in this field?

Since they were founded in the mid-1940s, the DGB unions have been the key players on the side of employees in German industrial relations. For a long time they had a monopoly of representation both vis-à-vis the political system and employers (Hassel 2007, p. 187). Over the past two decades, however, the expansion of the low-pay sector, the internal and external erosion of regional collective agreements,[2] as well as the rise of professional unions have changed the environment in which the DGB unions operate and take action. The transformation from trade associations to professional unions, which pursue an independent collective bargaining policy, especially in state-related or formerly state-owned sectors, has, over time, turned into new competition for the established DGB trade unions. The Federal Government and employers' associations also fear that the competition on the union side will put the system of social partnership under additional pressure (BDA 2010) although empirical studies have come to the conclusion that this trend has not yet put pressure on the model as a whole (Schroeder et al. 2011). Nevertheless, the state has developed additional stabilising measures through new laws in order to promote the social partnership-corporatist arrangement, in particular through the Collective Bargaining Act *(Tarifeinheitsgesetz)*.

Despite offering a wide range of activities and getting support from the state, the weakening of both the presence and effectiveness of German trade unions in almost all sectors and in almost all employee groups and regions could not be prevented. At the same time, differences between the unions have also intensified. German industrial relations can be subdivided into three more or less clearly defined worlds, which display fundamental differences and which have very little in common (ibid., p. 142). In the first world, especially in the export-oriented industry as well as in the public sector, there are collective actors who are organisationally strong in number and can enforce agreements. The second world, which exists mainly in peripheral areas of the manufacturing

---

2 According to Streeck/Rehder (2005), an internal and external erosion of the collective bargaining agreement is taking place: The reduction in the areas regulated by the collective bargaining policy is called external erosion, whereas internal erosion stands for the declining ability to standardise procedures, which is closely associated with using collective bargaining on the basis of so-called exemption clauses.

sector and in relatively well-developed service companies, is characterised by an ambivalence towards organisational policy. In the third world, which includes large parts of the basic services sector, trade and – regionally speaking – east Germany, both the unions and the employers' associations are barely represented. In particular, those service sectors which employ mostly women have become increasingly more union-free in recent years (Hassel 2007, p. 184).

For some years, we have observed a trend towards disorganisation, especially in the service sector, in trade and in some regions which are associated with a variety of other crisis symptoms. The central issue of membership development is not simply that DGB unions have continuously lost members since the 1980s (Ebbinghaus/Göbel 2014). Equally important are the structural difficulties faced by the trade unions; having to adapt to the changing business environment and labour market structures in order to prevent the existing representation gaps from getting worse. Since the 1980s, employers see unions ever less in the role of partners with whom they negotiate and cooperate. One result of these processes, which are accompanied by a decline in trade-union power resources, is the unions' declining strength to enforce agreements, which is clearly reflected in changes to the collective bargaining system (flexibilisation, decentralisation, lack of collective bargaining).

In this article, we start from the assumption that unions can definitely influence their own strength by establishing their own strategic membership policy. In this sense, we argue that it is necessary to find new approaches, which build on existing structures and reinforce the directions the unions have already pursued. The article is divided into two main parts: The first part is based on data from the European Social Survey (ESS)[3] and the membership data collected by the DGB trade unions. We trace the membership developments of the DGB unions and analyse the socio-structural dimensions of union members. In the second part, we discuss current trade union strategies in the area of membership policies. As an example, reference is made to the organising projects of the metal sector union IG Metall, which deal with a systematic reform of member structures within the existing organisational context. Next, through the example of employee/member surveys we examine how, by taking member preferences into consideration, internal and external legitimacy can be generated using thematic priorities or involving collective bargaining partners. In the thematic reorientation in member policies discussed here, we see attempts to strengthen social partnership in Germany, which, in many ways, has become rather fragile.

---

3   The unionisation levels shown below, based on the European Social Survey (ESS) (2017) with the wave of surveys carried out between 2002 and 2016, refer to the ratio of members in a union or similar organisation (Variable mbtru).

2 Membership and Representation Gaps

As membership organisations, trade unions rely on a broad membership base to not only provide the financial basis for their services and level of performance, but also to generate the basis for their legitimacy, representation, mobilisation and, ultimately, for collective bargaining and socio-political assertiveness. In this respect, the fact that the number of union members in the DGB unions has halved since the 1990s *(figure 1)*, while the workforce has reached a historic high, is a serious and complex problem.

In 2017, the degree of unionisation in the DGB was 15.0%. According to the ESS data, which incorporates all trade unions and trade union organisations, and has the advantage of offering a better international comparison, the level of unionisation[4] in Germany in 2016 was 20.7%.[5] This means that unionisation in Germany is well below the level of organisation of many countries in the European Union. The degree of union organisation is particularly high in countries where unions have been granted seemingly public administration responsibilities in the field of unemployment insurance (Belgium, Sweden, Finland, Denmark) *(table 1;* Ebbinghaus et al. 2011). The comparison between 2002 and 2016 almost always shows a decline in the degree of organisation (with the exception of Belgium and Norway), which can also be observed in the Nordic countries (Sweden –3.9%, Finland –4.0%).

While we work with the ESS data for a European comparison, we can use the membership data reported by the unions for the analysis of developments in Germany. In addition to the generally declining membership development, there are very different developments in individual sectors; differences between the export-oriented and the domestic-oriented sectors are especially prominent, as are the unions in the public sector. While there is a greater capacity for action in the export-oriented sector, which is mainly represented by the chemical and mineworkers' union IG BCE *(Industriegewerkschaft Bergbau, Chemie, Energie)* and IG Metall, unionisation levels in state-orientated trade unions in the education sector and the police have increased in recent years *(figure 2)*.

Firstly, when looking at the development since 2001, it can be seen that German trade unions, as a whole, are struggling with a decline in membership. Secondly, the

---

4   In order to ensure a consistency in the international comparative data, the following explanations are based, in particular, on the ESS data (survey 2002 and 2016) (for a comparison, also see the study by Schnabel/Wagner 2006). Studies that are confined to Germany usually refer to the General Population Survey of the Social Sciences (ALLBUS) (e.g. Schnabel 2005; Schnabel/Wagner 2003, 2007; Biebeler/Lesch 2007) or the Socio-Economic Panel (SOEP) (e.g. Fitzenberger et al. 2011) and particularly take into account, in their studies, the socio-structural characteristics of employees.

5   To measure the level of organisation, persons are only taken into account, who were actively employed at the time of the survey (union member ESS variable mbtru = 1, "1. Yes, currently" [actively employed] 2002 ESS variable empl = 1; 2016 ESS variable emplrel = 1 & mnactic = 1).

FIGURE 1

Number of members and union density^A in German trade unions, 1950–2017

Results in million (left scale) and as a percentage (right scale)

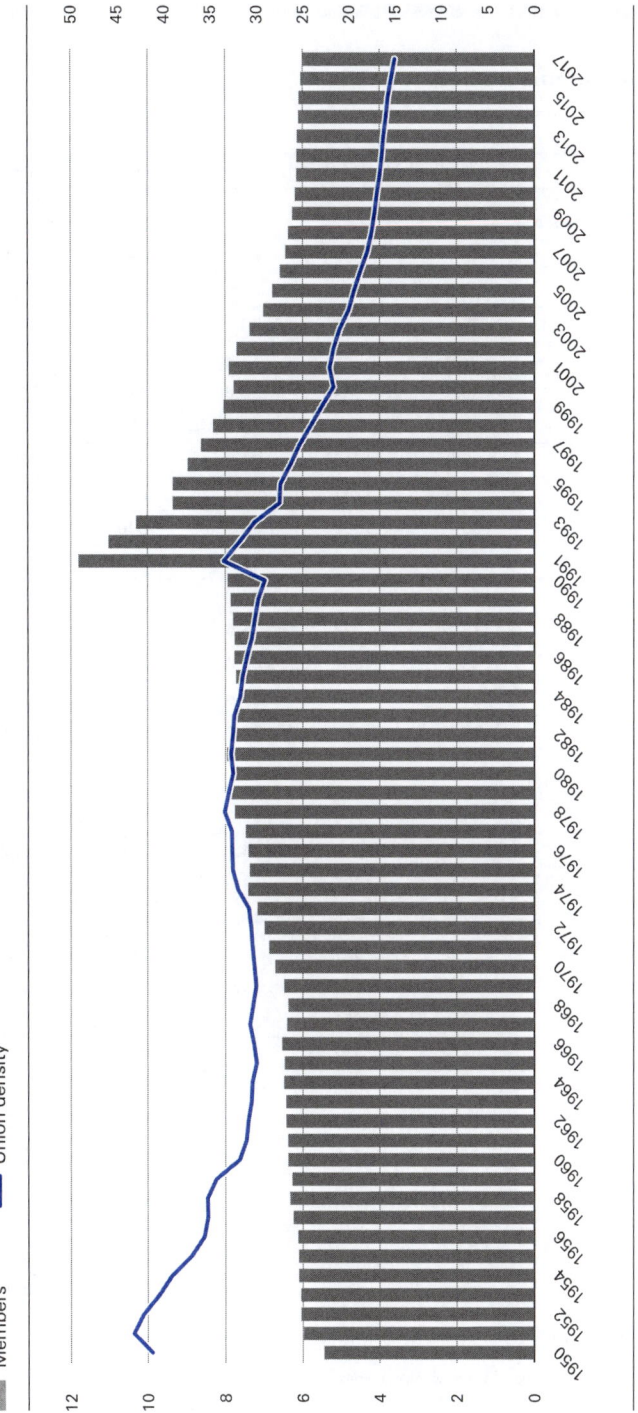

A Own calculations and description

Source: DGB 2018; Statistisches Bundesamt; Greef 2014

TABLE 1

Trade union members in Europe[A]

Results in absolute numbers and as a percentage

	% Total	N = 100 %	% Male	N = 100 %	% Female	N = 100 %
2002						
Belgium	43.7	869	46.6	498	40.1	356
Germany	22.3	1322	29.9	678	14.5	644
Finland	77.5	921	70.6	453	84.2	468
France	12.6	667	13.8	324	11.4	343
Great Britain	30.1	984	28.6	473	31.6	511
Ireland	40.8	888	45.0	422	37.0	466
Netherlands	28.9	1215	34.3	601	23.5	614
Norway	59.6	1261	57.2	677	62.4	584
Austria	35.7	1096	42.3	540	29.1	556
Poland	20.7	694	18.5	384	23.6	310
Sweden	78.3	1102	74.8	573	82.0	529
Switzerland	18.2	1097	21.5	557	14.7	540
Slovenia	49.1	662	43.8	334	54.4	328
Czech Republic	21.8	580	21.8	302	22.1	275
Country average	**38.5**		**39.2**		**37.9**	
2016						
Belgium	51.2	709	52.0	358	50.4	351
Germany	20.7	1322	24.1	730	16.4	592
Finland	73.5	785	67.6	407	79.9	378
France	12.9	825	14.7	403	11.1	422
Great Britain	25.6	821	22.7	369	27.9	452
Ireland	28.4	1069	24.9	535	31.8	534
Netherlands	22.4	651	24.6	288	20.7	363
Norway	63.6	817	55.9	451	73.0	366
Austria	27.4	1006	31.9	478	23.3	528
Poland	10.6	666	8.5	347	12.9	319
Sweden	74.4	742	69.2	367	79.4	375
Switzerland	13.0	753	13.2	403	12.9	350
Slovenia	28.6	516	26.0	264	31.3	252
Czech Republic	8.1	1152	9.1	586	7.0	566
Country average	**32.9**		**31.7**		**34.1**	

A   Level of organisation of active workers, for a comparison, see footnote 5

WSI Mitteilungen

Quelle: European Social Survey 2017; own calculations

police union GdP *(Gewerkschaft der Polizei)* and education union GEW *(Gewerkschaft Erziehung und Wissenschaft)* succeeded in reversing this development and moved towards a structurally positive growth trend. The situation is different with the railway union EVG *(Eisenbahn- und Verkehrsgewerkschaft,* formerly *Transnet),* which operates in a formerly state-owned but now privatised environment and finds itself facing a dynamic, competitive non-DGB affiliate union *(Gewerkschaft Deutscher Lokomotivführer,*

FIGURE 2

Membership development of German trade unions[A]

Results as a percentage

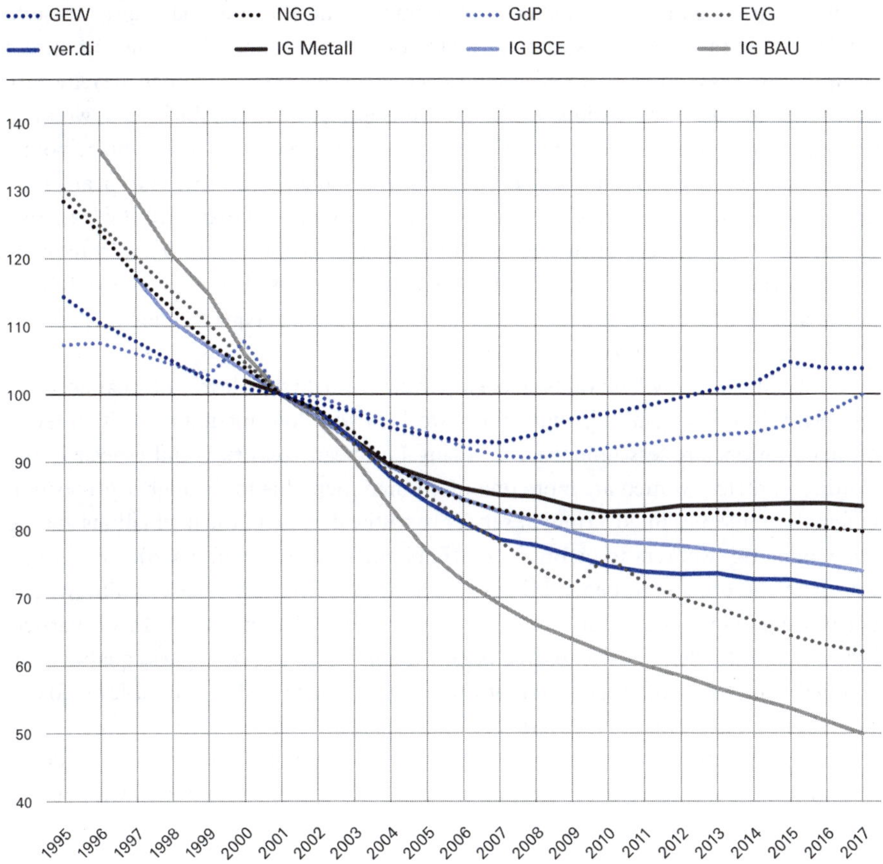

····· GEW ···· NGG ····· GdP ····· EVG
—— ver.di —— IG Metall —— IG BCE —— IG BAU

A Figure 2 shows the membership development of individual trade unions in Germany.
As an index value = 100 refers to the year 2001, which is to be seen as the conclusion of a phase
of trade union mergers, with the founding of ver.di.

Source: DGB 2018; own calculations and description

GDL). The EVG, along with the construction sector union IG BAU *(Industriegewerk-schaft Bauen-Agrar-Umwelt)*, forms a group of unions that are confronted with a significant (in percentage) decline in membership and the accompanying reduction in their finances. The EVG laments the fact that they have seen a reduction of 40 % in members, compared to membership in 2001, at IG BAU there has even been a reduction of around 50 %. Thirdly, there is a middle group of trade unions (metal sector union IG Metall, restaurant and food union NGG *[Gewerkschaft Nahrung-Genuss-Gaststätten]*, service sector union ver.di *[Vereinte Dienstleistungsgewerkschaft]*, chemical sector union IG BCE), which, although faced with a decline in membership, have succeeded in partially stopping it and significantly slowing down membership decline.

The international comparison *(table 1)* shows that the trend towards a decline in membership is taking place in almost all countries, and thus the challenges are quite similar. At the same time, it is particularly the experiences of Nordic trade unions that show that success can be achieved among salaried employees and women, despite part-time work and partly precarious working conditions. By contrast, the level of women's unionisation in Germany is 7.7 percentage points and in Austria 8.6 percentage points lower than that of men. Not only is this difference smaller in other European trade unions, but in many countries women are even more organised than men *(table 1)*. This means that socio-structural change and the resultant decline in traditional core membership groups do not necessarily lead to membership losses. At the same time, it must be noted that organisational successes in 'new' social groups require different approaches, incentives and strategies.[6]

While workers, civil servants and employees with higher levels of qualifications are relatively well-organised, white-collar workers with low, medium and high levels of qualifications are less unionised. In many European countries, and especially the Nordic countries, women are more unionised than men, due to the higher proportion of female employees in government services and the decline in the inclinations among male industrial workers to be organised (Ebbinghaus et al. 2009, p.349). By contrast, Germany and other continental European countries continue to face a significant gender-based gap in mobilisation and representation (Hassel 2007, p.182). This is particularly clear in the degree of employee organisation, based on the highest qualification attained. The degree of organisation of women with low to middle school-level qualifications is significantly lower than that of men *(figure 3)*.

The gender-specific differences with regard to the type of employment contract are also striking. Thus, there is a much higher degree of organisation for men with perma-

---

6   At this point, reference should be made to the literature study by Knyphausen-Aufseß et al. (2010), especially pp. 568ff., which systematically maps out the different determinants of union membership in the relevant publications between 2001 and 2010. In doing so, they come to the conclusion that the influencing characteristics can be subdivided into five categories: 1. personal characteristics, 2. employment characteristics, 3. operational characteristics, 4. attitudes and opinions and 5. the social environment (ibid., p.571).

nent and full-time contracts. Significant deficits, however, are found for women in both cases, whose degree of organisation is 8 to 9 % lower *(figure 4)*.

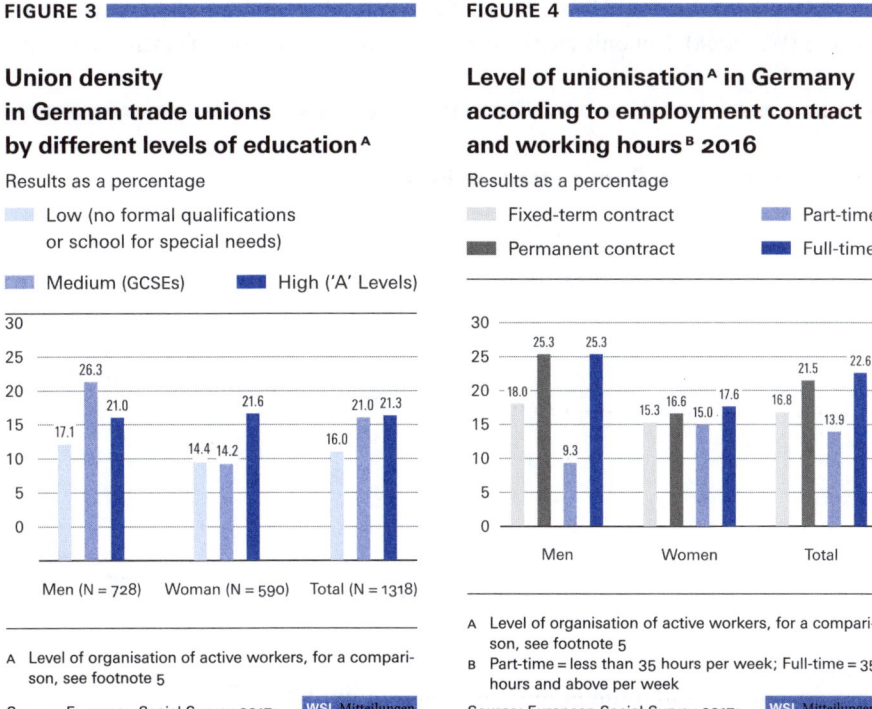

FIGURE 3

Union density in German trade unions by different levels of education[A]

Results as a percentage

Low (no formal qualifications or school for special needs)

Medium (GCSEs)　High ('A' Levels)

Men (N = 728)　Woman (N = 590)　Total (N = 1318)

A Level of organisation of active workers, for a comparison, see footnote 5

Source: European Social Survey 2017; own calculations and description

WSI Mitteilungen

FIGURE 4

Level of unionisation[A] in Germany according to employment contract and working hours[B] 2016

Results as a percentage

Fixed-term contract　Part-time

Permanent contract　Full-time

Men　Women　Total

A Level of organisation of active workers, for a comparison, see footnote 5
B Part-time = less than 35 hours per week; Full-time = 35 hours and above per week

Source: European Social Survey 2017; own calculations and description

WSI Mitteilungen

The established structures of the trade unions in industry also reflect the different labour market participation of women, especially within the industrial and service sectors *(figure 5)*. The trade union mergers, which began in the 1990s, have turned trade unions into multi-sectoral organisations, however, there have not been any structural changes in gender-specific levels of organisation. One exception is IG BAU, which displays an increase in its share of women, from around 12 % in 1996 to 26 % in 2017. This can be attributed to changes in the structure of the sector (particularly due to the integration and growth of the cleaning industry).

The proportion of women in ver.di, NGG and the GEW is significantly higher than that of industrial unions or the GdP or EVG. However, the increasing labour market participation of women is barely noticeable in the development in membership of the individual unions. As an example, reference is made to IG BCE, which increased its share of women from 1997 (19 %) to 2017 (21.5 %) by 2.5 %, or IG Metall, whose share of women remained unchanged between 2000 and 2017 at around 18 % (ibid.).

Most private sector unions and individual service sectors have remained classic male domains, despite a certain upward trend since the 1970s; for 25 years, the proportion of women in the unions remained unchanged at about one third. By contrast, the female employment rate increased by 15.7 % over the same period, from 54.9 % in 1993 to 70.6 % in 2016 (WSI 2018). Not only are there still shortcomings in women's membership, but

FIGURE 5

Female members in German trade unions

Results as a percentage

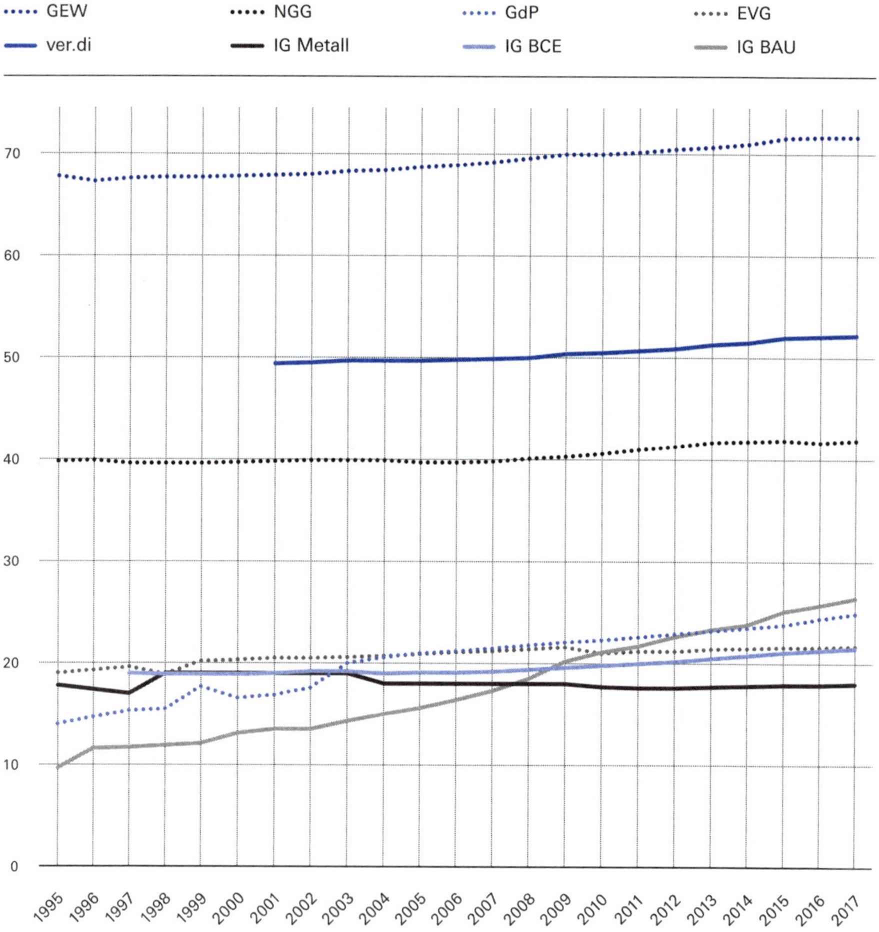

····· GEW ····· NGG ····· GdP ····· EVG
—— ver.di —— IG Metall —— IG BCE —— IG BAU

Source: DGB 2018; own calculations and description

also in the proportion of female elected representatives and the representation of women's interests. Although there was an increase in the number of female elected representatives in the works council to 39 % (2015), following the amendment of the Works Constitution Act *(Betriebsverfassungsgesetz, BetrVG)* in 2001, there is still a significant deficit in representation (Baumann et al. 2017). As a result, women are often absent in leadership positions at the company level.

Trade unions are not only behind the times when it comes to the gender distribution of their membership. Also where age is concerned, union membership does not reflect the reality in the labour markets. In 2016, the share of 16 to 30-year-olds in the labour market was 19.5 % and 51 to 65-year-olds made up 29.1 %. By contrast, only 15.3 % of union members were 16 to 30 years old, but 25.4 % were between 51 and 65 years old.

Over time, the level of unionisation of young people up to the age of 30 has remained almost unchanged in the past few years, however, the figure is very low *(table 2)*. The reasons for this are the fact that young people spend more time in education, often have atypical employment contracts at the start of their careers and work in sectors and companies with hardly any trade union presence. However, general trends towards individualisation and changing values among young people play a role here (Ebbinghaus/Goebel 2014, pp. 225ff.). This weak inclination to be organised at a young age is also problematic because of the long-term consequences; if young people fail to enter a trade union at the beginning of their working life, they are unlikely to do so later on, as willingness to join a trade union tends to decrease with age.

Company size plays a key role in the likelihood of employees becoming union members. The level of unionisation in 2016 was 10.3 % for companies with less than 100 employees, 19.1 % for companies with 100 to 499 employees and as high as 27.1 % for companies with more than 500 employees (European Social Survey 2017). One of the reasons for this is that the larger a company, the more likely it is that there will be a works council and shop stewards and, therefore, a climate, which makes the recruitment of members easier. In fact, the degree of organisation is highest in large companies that are covered by a collective bargaining agreement. In addition to the workplace-related arguments, societal and social aspects also play an important role. Having social contact with union members in one's family, within a circle of friends or at the workplace improves conditions for membership, whether it be through someone

TABLE 2

Level of organisation of German trade unions in different age groups[A]

Results in absolute numbers and as a percentage

Age groups	2002		2016	
	%	N = 100 %	%	N = 100 %
16–30	15.0	244	15.3	234
31–40	19.9	371	18.7	283
41–50	23.8	387	20.5	321
51–65	29.7	303	25.4	473
66+	9.4	7	5.1	11

A Level of organisation of active workers, for a comparison, see footnote 5

Quelle: European Social Survey 2017; WSI Mitteilungen
own calculations

setting an example, peer pressure or increased access to information (Goerke/Pannenberg 2007; Ebbinghaus et al. 2009; for care of the elderly: Schroeder 2017). According to the "social custom theory", a weak trade union presence can also develop into a downward spiral; as union membership becomes scarce, the chances of having contact with a union member in one's immediate social environment are reduced, and so is the likelihood of taking up union membership.

3 Trade Union Membership Development Strategies

High levels of unionisation, as already explained at the outset with reference to the three world heuristics (Schroeder/Wessels 2003, p. 19), are concentrated primarily within the manufacturing sector, the public sector, larger companies and certain regions. The loss of members arises due to social and economic shifts. From the point of view of trade union recruitment policy, the membership crisis can be discussed from four perspectives:

- *Socio-structural:* as an erosion of the social milieus and as the emancipation (individualisation, the increased importance of profit margins and the loss of the binding effect) of employees compared to large social organisations.
- *Economic:* The benefits of union membership are evaluated differently and, in many cases, ignored completely. Today, more than ever, there is the impression that one's professional career is independent of large social organisations.
- *Political:* The traditional interest in participation, as a long-lasting, time-consuming and highly identifiable procedure, has declined significantly in recent years. Participation in existing forms of intra-organisational decision-making does not currently appear to provide an incentive for non-members to join. This raises the question of how the usefulness of trade unions can be improved for the individual, without jeopardising the feasibility of policies that show solidarity.
- *By the employer:* One subject that is under-researched is the declining interest of employers to promote trade unions as a regulative body and therefore to support union membership (Hassel 2014a).

Trade unions have responded to the decline in membership and shortfalls in efficiency in a number of ways over recent years. In addition to the obligatory reform and structural changes to their core policy areas, such as collective bargaining and operating policies, they have implemented five adjustment and stabilisation strategies:

(1) *Trade union mergers:* Since 1995, mergers have reduced the number of DGB unions from 16 to 8. It is worth noting that the two largest individual unions, IG Metall and ver.di, represent, with 70 %, over two-thirds of the individual DGB members.

(2) *Cost reduction:* The DGB and individual trade unions use business tools to reduce costs and increase efficiency. This includes the reduction of personnel and the development of a professionalised, knowledge-based provision of services, as well as cost-effective bureaucracy (Müller/Wilke 2014, pp. 154ff.). Another element in transforming the external architecture is abandoning the idea of nationwide coverage of trade union offices. This is accompanied by a loss of proximity to members; at the same time, this is an element of the transformation from a milieu organisation, which exists only in part, to a professionalised service organisation.

(3) *Focus on representation:* The work of the unions is increasingly focused on their "core business". Compared to earlier times, when the unions were involved in many political areas, they now usually only speak out in areas where they feel competent.

(4) *Focus on the state:* There is an increased focus on the state, which has, even in self-regulated tasks, such as collective bargaining, become more involved in trade union policy – from the minimum wage to supporting measures in collective bargaining policy. In this respect, unions are responding to the fact that their protection and transformative processes have not been adequate in covering all their members.

(5) *New membership policy:* Since the 1990s, there has been a strategic policy for recruiting and activating new member groups. On the one hand, the focus has been on weakly-organised groups, such as temporary workers or engineers. On the other hand, the task of recruiting members within the organisation is equipped with its own structures, resources, people and goals. Important suggestions for taking a proactive stand towards membership recruitment stem not only from the former retail and banking union HBV (which later merged into ver.di), but also from the US unions, who had achieved considerable success with their so-called "organising" (Wetzel 2013). Similar initiatives can be found in most trade unions. However, against the background of the decline in membership and organisational difficulties, unions are not only looking for ways to target specific groups in their membership recruitment, but are generally taking it as the starting point for a new organisational development policy.

Based on the problems with finding new members, which we identified above, we will consider the fifth action strategy (new membership policy) below. We will consider the strategic implementation of membership policies and methods of inquiry, bringing to the fore two currently under-researched phenomena for future trade union action. We focus our observations on IG Metall, in the knowledge that some of the practices outlined here have been tried previously in other unions.

3.1 New Membership Policy

Trade unions have, in the past, developed a variety of activities and strategies specific to target groups; "selective incentives" and tools to make them more attractive to different groups of workers. Up to now, these specific activities have mostly been designed as individual measures that have had very little structural impact on the overall organisation (goals, structures and instruments), even if they were successful. This has changed in recent years, as IG Metall, for example, has been attempting to operate a strategic readjustment of its recruitment policy since 2007. In addition to its own local pilot projects and suggestions from other DGB unions, significant incentives for this change were taken from the Anglo-Saxon countries in particular, both through trade union research and through direct exchange between German unions and internationally associated trade unions (Frege 2000; Schreieder 2005; Bremme et al. 2007; Woodruff 2007; Schmalstieg 2010). In developing this further, it is possible to present a project structure that progresses in stages, whose initial focus was primarily on collecting initial, practical experience of its own and a systematic approach to gaining members. As things progressed with the first sector-wide organising project in the wind energy industry (2010–2012) and the establishment of a considerable "investment fund", to finance a larger number of regional projects, activities increasingly focused on teaching new approaches to IG Metall's control structure (Boewe/Schulten 2013; Dribbusch 2013; Goes et al. 2015; IGM Vorstand 2015).

3.2 Development Projects at IG Metall: Strategic Membership Policy

Against the background of sharply reduced numbers of members, IG Metall sought a strategy of its own in order to integrate members, foster participation and deal with conflict. With some preliminary work already having begun in the late 1980s, a systematic, district-based development strategy, based on projects spanning nine years, was finally started in 2015. The basic support structure of the development projects is a group of *organisers*, who act as so-called "development officers", operating in cooperation with company activists – and in cases where such activists are absent, themselves pursue the recruitment of members. When taking all districts into consideration, about 140 activists were hired, who were expected to be able to handle and control the range of membership issues, participation and local conflicts and move between companies and local union offices. The specific concept of the development strategy puts the onus on the districts, which set their own precedents and contexts according to their own priorities within a given nationwide framework.

The new projects have the task of attracting more members and generating better methods, tools and structures for membership development. The latter should also have institutional implications for work in local trade union offices, especially where they interface with companies. It is particularly important that this structure allows insights to be gained which enable an increase in the effectiveness of membership recruitment and make it possible that what is learned can be transferred into the organisational structure of regular work. It is not just about attracting members; it is also about organisational and cultural change that helps the organisation to tailor its proposals to workers' needs. One aspect of the strategy is participation-oriented approaches.

3.3 Member Surveys

The orientation towards members can be described as a twofold transformation process by trade unions. On the one hand, unions align their organisation more purposefully towards people who are (not yet) members and establish more professional forms of recruitment, mentoring and commitment. To this aim, new structures, actors and investments in the area of member recruitment need to be established. On the other hand, the strategic "reorientation" of unions may also result in granting members other forms of participation. In this respect, the content and legitimacy of the role of members has changed almost parallel with the modified organisational set-up. This includes concrete ways for increased member orientation in collective bargaining mobilisation processes, such as concepts of investment-oriented/company-oriented collective bargaining policy; the principle of "organising through conflict" or the policy that a company collective agreement, for example, can only be negotiated when a company has a certain degree of organisation. From an analytical perspective, the DGB trade unions are responding, in this way, to the lack of new members, new competition and a declining assertiveness by strengthening the logic of membership over the logic of influence (Schmitter/Streeck 1981). In trying to balance out the tension between the two logics, unions have, for a long time, focused on promoting their interests and influence to the outside world, thus relying on their assertiveness due to their corporate involvement. With the new focus on membership recruitment and retention, but also with the conflict-oriented activation approach, the logic of membership level is increasingly being addressed. With greater direct focus on the interests of members, unions are again focusing more on their primary source of power: their members.

Employee or member surveys play an important role, in addition to a wide variety of activation methods within the framework of pay and company-specific conflicts. These have been used more systematically for several years. While such surveys have occasionally been used in the past to give the board of directors a kind of secret insight into the state of the organisation, they are now openly communicated and used as an instrument for intra-organisational discussions, on the one hand, in order to more transparently clarify basic questions as regards content or organisational development but also to ensure that collective bargaining goals reflect the preferences of members and employees in the sector and, therefore, to establish a basis of legitimacy that goes beyond the internal trade union committees. *Table 3* presents some key surveys that follow this formula for a new legitimacy policy.

These standardised surveys enable a collation of the preferences of members in order to set priorities and better substantiate their demands. To date, the employee and member surveys used in the trade unions do not have the status of a regular and binding source of legitimacy in order to prepare collective bargaining agreements. Rather, they support the work of the union board and collective bargaining committees by providing additional sources of knowledge, communication and legitimacy. However, with their direct reference to their members' perceptions, interests and preferences, they must also be classified as building blocks in an interest-oriented and direct democracy within the trade unions. What is decisive, however, is that these references are not a substitute for, but additional to, the structures and processes of representative democracy within the organisation. Nevertheless, they constitute a limitation to the agenda-setting power of committees. By capturing workers' preferences more authentically than through communication processes, based only on committees within the organisation, these surveys are also an additional source of mobilisation and legitimacy for employers, policymakers and the public. This more direct and broad commitment to the specific interests of members seeks to take into account the interests of the participants, on the one hand, and, on the other hand, improve the association's assertiveness when dealing with employers and policymakers.

4 Conclusion: Redefinition of Trade Union Work as a Basis for New Social Partnership

In the concept of a social market economy and conflict partnership (Müller-Jentsch), the notion of two equal sides of a power dispute plays an outstanding role within the framework of collective bargaining autonomy. This configuration of negotiations between equals, which is far removed from both the state and companies, presupposes organisational power on both sides, which has no longer been the reality, and certainly not in all areas, due to the dramatic decline in the membership of social partners since the 1980s. With a degree of unionisation of around 15 %, the German trade unions, as shown in international comparison, have a below-average level of organisation, which is declining more dramatically in comparison to other countries. Nonetheless, in the manufacturing sector, in the civil service and in larger companies, there are still mostly high levels of unionisation and effective employers' associations. But, even in the metal industry, collective bargaining, which correlates to the degree of organisation, has been declining since 1990. IG Metall has used this fact as an opportunity to make the commitment to membership and collective bargaining the central reference point for their own structural reorganisation (Hofmann 2016, pp. 143).

The organising power of trade unions is seen as a primary requirement for practising the complex procedure of cooperation and opposition between trade unions and employers' organisations. In the German model, a conflicting situation has developed in industrial relations in the manufacturing industry and the service sector: While social

TABLE 3

German trade union members surveys

Gewerkschaft	IG Metall			IG BCE		EVG	GdP
Title	Your vote for a good life	Work: safe and fair!	Politics for everyone – safe, fair and self-determined	The IG BCE youth study	Inside the IG BCE	Together more! Wage negotiations 2016	Member survey 2004
Time frame	4–6.2009	2–4.2013	1–2.2017	5.2011–6.2012	4–5.2016	8–9.2016	1–2.2004
Interviewees	Non-/Members	Non-/Members	Non-/Members	Non-/Members (15 to 29 years old)	Members	Members	Members
Number of interviewees	451899 747 firms	514134 ~8400 firms	681241 ~7000 firms	2735	1300 (representative)	~15000	1532 (representative)
Objective	Demands directed at new Federal Government	Demands directed at new Federal Government	Preparations for wage negotiations	Interests and representation of young people	Evaluation of member satisfaction	Preparations for wage negotiations	Mood on the reform policy of the Federal Government
Themes	Pensions Justice Good work Minimum wages Compatibility Securing the future	Age-appropriate jobs Flexibility Change of course Minimum wages Compatibility Further education	Pensions Working hours Justice Integration Qualifications Self-determination Compatibility Further education	Education Participation Pay Shortage of skills Good work Safety Further education Future of work	Work priorities Co-termination Member support	Working hours Pay Pensions Further education Qualifications	Pensions Civil service Pay Health insurance Working life Long-term planning Right to strike
Policy Fields	Society politics Social policy	Labour market policy Management policy Society politics	Labour market policy Social policy Collective bargaining policy	Collective bargaining policy Membership policy	Membership policy	Collective bargaining policy	Social policy Collective bargaining policy

Source: own compilation

partnership in the industrial sector can survive without any significant major conflicts, the service sector is characterised by many conflicts and is without a stable social partnership structure (Streeck 2016; Schroeder 2016). The practice of social partnership in the manufacturing sector is based on potentially conflictive actors, who express this ability to mobilise in their daily, professional activities and in many smaller conflicts, and whose bargaining power, in particular, can be seen to have creative elements. Thus, in spite of intensifying globalisation, a central part of the German economy continues to be characterised by a basically conflictual partnership structure, which at the same time results in a certain structuring of the political economy as an export-oriented organisation of its institutions (Hassel 2014b, p. 138). However, without structural changes, this constellation in the field of industrial relations cannot simply be updated, on the contrary more fundamental change is necessary.

The trade unions have long been aware of representation gaps in the areas of female employees, the highly-skilled and, increasingly, among younger employees and have tried to provide answers through a variety of initiatives. But so far, all these measures have been insufficient to create any noticeable reversal of this trend. Despite individual DGB affiliated unions being able to stop their membership decline, in 2017 the DGB fell short of its "magic limit" of 6 million members. Our thesis here is that, so far, a strategic membership policy, which would have to be characterised by its own resources, rules and boards of directors, has yet to materialise. IG Metall has systematically embedded the aforementioned points in recent years (see section 3.2), and the process is still ongoing. A separate policy field, dealing with membership policy, which would be responsible not only for the recruitment of members, but also for retaining membership and other activities related to membership policy, would have to be assimilated in the fields of collective bargaining and company policy. This would probably establish a more dynamic and effective policy, which would also generate membership-related, in other words participation-oriented, feedback in other policy areas.

Trade unions are the key to the future of social partnership. Support from the state, and even more so the insight of companies and their associations that trade unions are important partners, should not be underestimated for stable industrial relations and a resilient social market economy. But all of this cannot disguise the fact that, without structurally sustainable changes in union membership policy, the accompanying policies of the state and employers are inadequate. Therefore, trade union activities towards building a more professional, strategic membership policy, their orientation towards participation and their new activities, and establishing tools for direct democracy, all build an important basis towards securing and developing their role in a political and economic democracy.

REFERENCES

Baumann, H. / Brehmer, W. / Hobler, D. / Klenner, Ch. / Pfahl, S. (2017): Frauen und Männer in Betriebsräten. Zur Umsetzung des Minderheitenschutzes bei Betriebsratswahlen, Wirtschafts- und Sozialwissenschaftliches Institut: WSI-Report Nr. 34, 01/2017, Düsseldorf

BDA (Bundesvereinigung der Deutschen Arbeitgeberverbände) (ed.) (2010): Arbeitgeberpräsident Dr. Dieter Hundt: Funktionsfähigkeit der Tarifautonomie gesetzlich sichern, Presse-Information Nr. 029/2010 of 23 June 2010

Biebeler H. / Lesch H. (2007): Zwischen Mitgliedererosion und Ansehensverlust: Die deutschen Gewerkschaften im Umbruch, in: Industrielle Beziehungen 14 (2), pp. 133–153

Boewe, J. / Schulten, J. (2013): Eine erfolgreiche Zumutung. Organizing in der Windkraftindustrie: Die Innenperspektive der IG Metall, in: Wetzel, D. (ed.): Organizing. Die Veränderung der gewerkschaftlichen Praxis durch das Prinzip Beteiligung, Hamburg, pp. 119–126

Bremme, P. / Fürniß, U. / Meinecke, U. (eds.) (2007): Never work alone. Organizing – ein Zukunftsmodell für Gewerkschaften, Hamburg

DGB (Deutscher Gewerkschaftsbund) (2018): Die Mitglieder der DGB-Gewerkschaften, http://www.dgb.de/uber-uns/dgb-heute/mitgliederzahlen (accessed 09 April 2018)

Dribbusch, H. (2013): Nachhaltig erneuern. Aufbau gewerkschaftlicher Interessenvertretung im Windanlagenbau, in: Wetzel, D. (ed.): Organizing. Die Veränderung der gewerkschaftlichen Praxis durch das Prinzip Beteiligung, Hamburg, pp. 92–118

Ebbinghaus, B. / Göbel, C. / Koos, S. (2009): Inklusions- und Exklusionsmechanismen gewerkschaftlicher Mitgliedschaft – ein europäischer Vergleich, in: Stichweh, R. / Windolf, P. (eds.): Inklusion und Exklusion. Analysen zur Sozialstruktur und sozialen Ungleichheit, Wiesbaden, pp. 341–359

Ebbinghaus, B. / Göbel, C. / Koos, S. (2011): Social capital, 'Ghent' and work-place contexts matter. Comparing union membership in Europe, in: European Journal of Industrial Relations 17 (2), pp. 107–124

Ebbinghaus, B. / Göbel, C. (2014): Mitgliederrückgang und Organisationsstrategien deutscher Gewerkschaften, in: Schroeder, W. (ed.): Handbuch Gewerkschaften in Deutschland, Wiesbaden, pp. 207–237

European Social Survey (ed.) (2017): Survey Data, http://nesstar.ess.nsd.uib.no/webview (accessed: 09 April 2018)

Fitzenberger, B. / Kohn, K. / Wang, Q. (2011): The erosion of union membership in Germany. Determinants, densities, decompositions, in: Journal of Population Economics 24 (1), pp. 141–165

Frege, C. M. (2000): Gewerkschaftsreformen in den USA. Eine kritische Analyse des ‚Organisationsmodells', in: Industrielle Beziehungen 7 (3), pp. 260–280

Goes, T. / Schmalz, S. / Thiel, M. / Dörre, K. (2015): Gewerkschaften im Aufwind? Stärkung gewerkschaftlicher Organisationsmacht in Ostdeutschland, Otto Brenner Stiftung: OBS-Arbeitsheft 83, Frankfurt a. M.

Goerke, L. / Pannenberg, M. (2007): Trade union membership and works councils in west Germany, in: Industrielle Beziehungen 14 (2), pp. 154–175

Greef, S. (2014): Gewerkschaften im Spiegel von Zahlen, Daten und Fakten, in: Schroeder, W. (ed.): Handbuch Gewerkschaften in Deutschland, Wiesbaden, pp. 657–755

Hassel, A. (2007): The curse of institutional security, in: Industrielle Beziehungen 14 (2), pp. 176–191

Hassel, A. (2014a): Trade unions and the future of democratic capitalism, in: Beramedia, P. / Häusermann, S. / Kitschelt, H. / Kriesi, H. (eds.): The politics of advanced capitalism, Cambridge, pp. 231–256

Hassel, A. (2014b): The German model in transition, in: Padgett, S. / Paterson, W. / Zohlnhöfer, R. (eds.): Developments in German politics 4, Houndmills/Basingstoke, pp. 133–148

Hofmann, J. (2016): Tarifbindung – eine Frage der Gerechtigkeit, in: WSI-Mitteilungen 69 (2), pp. 143–147

IGM (IG Metall) Vorstand (ed.) (2015): Strategische Erschließung. Werkvertragsbeschäftigte organisieren sich! Beispiel eines Organizing-Projektes im Automobilcluster Leipzig, Frankfurt a. M.

Knyphausen-Aufseß, D. zu / Linke, R. / Nikol, P. (2010): Die deutschen Gewerkschaften: Ein Review der aktuellen Forschungsliteratur, in: Journal of Business Economics 80 (5), pp. 561–609

Müller, H.-P. / Wilke, M. (2014): Gewerkschaftsfusionen: der Weg zu modernen Multibranchengewerkschaften, in: Schroeder, W. (ed.): Handbuch Gewerkschaften in Deutschland, Wiesbaden, pp. 147–171

Schmalstieg, C. (2010): Lernen von den US-Gewerkschaften, in: Greef, S. / Kalass, V. / Schroeder, W. (eds.): Gewerkschaften und die Politik der Erneuerung – Und sie bewegen sich doch, Düsseldorf, pp. 207–225

Schmitter, P. C. / Streeck, W. (1981): The organization of business interests: A research design to study the associative action of business in the advanced industrial societies of Western Europe, Wissenschaftszentrum Berlin für Sozialforschung: WZB-Discussion Paper IIM/LMP 81/13

Schnabel, C. (2005): Gewerkschaften und Arbeitgeberverbände: Organisationsgrade, Tarifbindung und Einflüsse auf Löhne und Beschäftigung, in: Zeitschrift für Arbeitsmarktforschung 38 (2 and 3), pp. 181–196

Schnabel, C. / Wagner, J. (2003): Trade union membership in eastern and western Germany: convergence or divergence?, in: Applied Economics Quarterly 49 (3), pp. 213–232

Schnabel, C. / Wagner, J. (2006): Who are the workers who never joined a union? Empirical evidence from western and eastern Germany, in: Industrielle Beziehungen 13 (2), pp. 118–131

Schnabel, C. / Wagner, J. (2007): The persistent decline in unionization in western and eastern Germany, 1980–2004: What can we learn from a decomposition analysis? In: Industrielle Beziehungen 14 (2), pp. 118–132

Schreieder, A. (2005): Organizing – Gewerkschaften als soziale Bewegung, https://bayern.verdi.de/gruppen/vertrauensleute/++file++51d287056f6844333000155e/download/Organizing-Gewerkschaft_als_soziale_Bewegung.pdf (accessed 09 April 2018)

Schroeder, W. (2016): Konfliktpartnerschaft – still alive. Veränderter Konfliktmodus in der verarbeitenden Industrie, in: Industrielle Beziehungen 23 (3), pp. 374–392

Schroeder, W. (2017): Kollektives Beschäftigtenhandeln in der Altenpflege, Hans-Böckler-Stiftung: Study Nr. 373, Düsseldorf

Schroeder, W. / Kalass, V. / Greef, S. (2011): Berufsgewerkschaften in der Offensive. Vom Wandel des deutschen Gewerkschaftsmodells, Wiesbaden

Schroeder, W. / Wessels, B. (2003): Die Gewerkschaften in Politik und Gesellschaft der Bundesrepublik Deutschland. Ein Handbuch, Wiesbaden

Streeck, W. / Rehder, B. (2005): Institutionen im Wandel: Hat die Tarifautonomie eine Zukunft? In: Busch, H. W. / Frey, H. P. / Hüther, M. / Rehder, B. / Streeck, W. (eds.): Tarifpolitik im Umbruch, Cologne, pp. 49–82

Streeck, W. (2016): Von Konflikt ohne Partnerschaft zu Partnerschaft ohne Konflikt: Industrielle Beziehungen in Deutschland, in: Industrielle Beziehungen 23 (1), pp. 47–60

Statistisches Bundesamt (2018): Arbeitsmarkt, https://www.destatis.de/DE/ZahlenFakten/Indikatoren/LangeReihen/Arbeitsmarkt/lrerw014.html (13 August 2018)

Wetzel, D. (ed.) (2013): Organizing. Die Veränderung der gewerkschaftlichen Praxis durch das Prinzip Beteiligung, Hamburg, pp. 47–63

Woodruff, T. (2007): Gewerkschaftsaufbau in schwierigen Zeiten. Wie die SEIU zur Gewerkschaft mit den höchsten Mitgliederzuwächsen in den USA wurde, in: Bremme, P. / Fürniß, U. / Meinecke, U. (eds.): Never work alone. Organizing – ein Zukunftsmodell für Gewerkschaften, Hamburg, pp. 92–116

WSI (Wirtschafts- und Sozialwissenschaftliches Institut der Hans-Böckler-Stiftung) (2018): Erwerbstätigkeit. Erwerbstätigenquoten und Erwerbsquoten 1991–2016, https://www.boeckler.de/53509.htm (accessed 08 July 2018)

AUTHORS

ANKE HASSEL, Prof. Dr., Professor of Public Policy at the Hertie School of Governance, Berlin; from 2016 until 2019 Scientific Director of the Institute of Economics and Social Sciences (WSI) of the Hans-Böckler-Foundation. Main areas of work: industrial relations, labour market, social policy.

@ E-Mail: Hassel@hertie-school.org

WOLFGANG SCHROEDER, Prof. Dr., teaches Political Science at the University of Kassel and is Research Fellow at the Berlin Social Science Center (WZB). Main areas of research: party, trade union and welfare state research.

@ E-Mail: wolfgang.schroeder@uni-kassel.de

New Militancy
in a Changing Industrial Landscape

The Migration of Industrial Action to the German Service Sector

For decades industrial conflict in Germany was dominated by disputes in metal manufacturing. Apart from two national strikes in the public sector, strike action in the service sector was a phenomenon the public did not take much notice of. Since the mid-2000s this picture has completely changed. It is most often nurses, childcare workers, train drivers, clinicians and other service workers who dominate the headlines when industrial action brings their problems and demands to broader attention. The article sketches the changes in the industrial landscape against which the shift of militancy to the service sector has taken place and explores the specific features of industrial action in the service sector.

HEINER DRIBBUSCH

1 Introduction

In July 2015, nursing staff at the Berlin hospital Charité, one of the largest medical facilities in Europe, embarked on a strike under the slogan "More of us are better for everyone" (Hedemann et al. 2017). The strikers' core demand was for the hospital to increase the number of nursing positions and recruit new staff to help alleviate the burden of overwork suffered by nursing and care staff. The nationwide publicity generated by this action led to further strikes on the same issue at other hospitals in subsequent years, some of which lasted for several weeks, as at the Düsseldorf University Hospital in the summer of 2018. Disputes such as these exemplify a new and broad-based process that, since the mid-2000s, has focused public attention on the working lives of employees in such diverse service sector occupations as nursery nurses, aircrew, train drivers, doctors and nursing staff. Strike action in Germany in the second half of the twentieth century was largely dominated by the metalworking industry (Dribbusch 2007). Since 2005, however, the balance has shifted to the service sector in a process characterised by Bordogna and Cella (2002), drawing on Accornero (1985), as the "tertiarisation of conflict" (Dribbusch/Vandaele 2007; Lesch 2015). This development not only reflects an intensification of distributive conflicts in the service sector, but also demands by service workers for greater social recognition and esteem.

Post-war economic development in Germany was characterised by a long phase of rising incomes and consumption that was matched by a broad-based increase in workforce skills. Both phenomena were an expression of the fact that a large majority of the labour force was covered by collective bargaining during this period. This began to change in the second half of the 1980s when economic policymakers and companies developed new strategies in response to the crises of the 1970s. And following the short-lived "unification boom" of 1992/93, an entirely new dynamic emerged in which not only private but also public employers openly challenged long-established collectively-agreed arrangements and employment conditions. Provisions to relax the application of agreed standards (so-called "opening clauses") – traditionally an exception – became the norm. The liberalisation of financial markets combined with the neo-liberal social policies pursued by the red-green federal coalition government (1998–2005) marked further steps along this trajectory. For the service sector, the decisive moment was the privatisation of basic public services that began in the late 1980s and spread rapidly during the 1990s; this was followed by the proliferation of precarious and low-paid jobs following the reforms of the social insurance and tax regime introduced in 2003. By the early 2000s, the assaults on established collectively-agreed norms associated with these processes began to encounter increasingly frequent employee resistance. At the same time, these developments also generated considerable differences in the circumstances and experiences of service workers, enabling some groups to mount successful defences of their interests in a series of separate conflicts.

The years between 2006 and 2018, the period dealt with in this article, represent a fairly short slice of time, with fluctuations in overall strike activity (measured here in terms of days not worked), often the result of contingent factors, such as whether individual bargaining rounds, and their associated disputes, coincided in any one year. This applies, for example, to 2015, an "unusually intensive" phase of strike action (Artus 2017) that was remarkable for several instances of spectacular industrial action (see Dörre et al. 2016). As developments in 2016 and 2017 subsequently showed, this proved to be more the exception than the norm. In 2018, for the first time since the mid-2000s, there was a wave of one-day strikes in the metalworking industry that pushed up the overall volume of strike activity in that year. Considered more broadly, strikes remain rare in Germany and only a minority of employees participate in industrial action even in years characterised by a high level of disputes. In a survey conducted for the Hans-Böckler-Foundation in 2008, 80 % of respondents said that they had never participated in either a full or token strike (Bewernitz/Dribbusch 2014).[1] Nonetheless, industrial relations in Germany are not only indisputably becoming more conflictual but the pattern of industrial action is also changing. Strikes are becoming shorter but more

---

[1] The survey, carried out in April and May 2008, was based on a representative sample of 2000 people aged between 16 and 65 who, at that time, were either in dependent employment, unemployed or in vocational training.

frequent than in the 1970s and 1980s, with industrial action in branches and by workers that were generally regarded as not especially strike-prone during the second half of the twentieth century. The following article is concerned less with a small number of high-profile strikes but rather with the patterns, trends and main features that have characterised industrial action in the service sector since the mid-2000s.

Industrial conflicts take place within particular sets of power relations and under certain institutional and economic conditions (Dribbusch/Vandaele 2007; Silver 2003; Schmalz/Dörre 2014). These *influence,* but do not determine, the course of industrial disputes, the trajectory and outcome of which are shaped by complex interdependencies between employees (and their trade unions) and companies, employer associations and the state (Brookes 2018). All those involved in a strike are individual actors with their own views and sense-making processes. As a result, strikes taking place under similar conditions can follow quite divergent trajectories. Strikes in the service sector, examined in greater detail below, not only do not conform to a single pattern, but have taken many differing, and on occasions contradictory, courses (see Birke 2016). While some strikes are the expression of assertive self-confidence on the part of employees and their trade unions, many have been forced on workers when trying to resist overt employer attacks, some are a combination of both. At the same time, strike action can also be a process through which employees test out the power relationships between themselves and their employers (and their associations).

The article provides an overview of the union landscape in the service sector and a brief account of the major changes there which are the background for understanding the shift in the locus of industrial action (section 2). This is followed by an outline of the various quantitative measures of strike activity in the German service sector, focusing on strikes in the context of formal, principally industry-level, collective bargaining; informal stoppages at workplace level occasioned by local disputes are rarely public and difficult to trace (3). Section 4 offers a look at the qualitative aspects of strike action, such as the capacity to engage in industrial action, employee demands, and strike tactics. The article concludes with an outline of future prospects in this area (5).

2 Employees' Associations and Transformation Processes in the Service Sector

2.1 The Union Landscape

Collective bargaining in the service sector is largely dominated by the United Services Union *(Vereinte Dienstleistungsgewerkschaft, ver.di),* an affiliate of the German Confederation of Trade Unions *(Deutscher Gewerkschaftsbund, DGB).* With just under two million members in 2018, ver.di covers both private and public services. In the public sector, ver.di engages in single-table bargaining with another employee organisation; the German Civil Service Federation *(dbb beamtenbund und tarifunion, dbb)*. The dbb is a confederation of some 40 professional and sectoral unions claiming a total membership of 1.3 million, of which 920 000 are public civil servants *(Beamte)*. dbb affiliates are on average less strike-prone than DGB unions but do not abstain entirely from industrial action. A prominent dbb affiliate is the German Union of Train Drivers *(Gewerkschaft Deutscher Lokomotivführer, GDL*; 34 000 members) which called several national rail strikes in 2007 and 2014/2015. GDL is in fierce competition in the rail sector with the DGB affiliate, the Railway and Transport Union *(Eisenbahn- und Verkehrsgewerkschaft, EVG*; 190 000 members) which on 10 December 2018 brought rail transport in Germany to a complete standstill in a show of force with a five-hour walk-out. Other unions that have engaged in industrial action since the mid-2000s are the clinicians' union *Marburger Bund (MB)*, which organises some 120 000 doctors in public and private hospitals, the German Journalists Association *(Deutscher Journalisten-Verband, DJV)*, which has some 33 500 members and is the largest journalists' union in the print media, and the pilots' association *(Vereinigung Cockpit, VC)*, which had 9600 members in 2018. None of the latter three are affiliated to a national confederation.

2.2 The Transformation of the Service Sector

Before proceeding to offer an explanation as to why the service sector (and specifically its very diverse individual parts) has recently played a growing role in the overall pattern of strike activity, and continues to do so, some consideration needs to be given to the context for this new and higher propensity to engage in industrial action. Up until the 1990s, relatively few strikes occurred in the service sector. One significant factor for this was that, up until the early 1990s, basic public services were supplied by the state. Collective bargaining was largely centralised and dominated by the then public services trade union ÖTV *(Gewerkschaft Öffentliche Dienste, Transport und Verkehr)* (see Keller 1993). One distinctive feature of the public sector in Germany is that employees who have been given the status of *Beamte,* equivalent to public servants in the UK, are not permitted to engage in collective bargaining; rather, their employment conditions and remuneration *(Besoldung,* literally 'stipend') is set by German legislatures at federal and regional *(Land)* level depending on their area of activity. Legal opinion generally holds that they are not entitled to strike.[2] One consequence of this was that, prior to privatisation, in addition to police officers and employees in the public education service (teachers, lecturers and professors), many employees performing non-executive roles in the public sector, such as staff at the Federal Postal Service *(Bundespost)* or Federal Railways *(Bundesbahn)*, were classified as *Beamte*; before 1990, this included all train drivers, for example.

---

2   The prohibition on strike action by *Beamte* was expressly reaffirmed by the Federal Constitutional Court in June 2018.

The main base for the ÖTV was therefore workers in the public transport, utilities and refuse disposal services provided by local government. To draw on a metaphor coined by Walter Müller-Jentsch (1997, p. 12), the ÖTV leadership saw the strike weapon principally as a "sword on the wall", something to be pointed to in negotiations but only rarely removed from its mountings. The sole instances of national-level strikes were in 1974 (for four days) and 1992 (for eleven days). And precisely because they were so rare, such strikes garnered enormous public interest and mobilised a large number of employees. The material foundation for this relatively low propensity to strike was the fact that public sector wages, although lower than those in industry, generally increased at a steady pace, with public employees enjoying job security and a reliable pension.

By contrast, the relatively low levels of strike activity in private services were a function of the very limited capacity of private service trade unions to engage in industrial action. Low levels of union membership meant that strikes were either effectively ruled out as a negotiating option or confined to short and limited actions. In addition, up until the 1990s, the employer side did not generally challenge the existence of collective bargaining in the main private services sectors and the improvements obtained through bargaining in industry were generally transmitted to the service sector, albeit with some lags and typically not in full.

The current situation is the outcome of a number of fundamental changes in the organisation and provision of services, the most profound of which was the political decision to transform the public sector into an area of service provision based on marketised relationships. The privatisation and liberalisation of post services and rail transport in the late 1980s was followed by local transport and other locally-provided services, and finally health services (see Böhlke 2009). This was compounded by an approach to tax and social policy that deprived local authorities of resources. All these changes progressively stripped away the foundations of the social partnership that had characterised public sector industrial relations (Kädtler 2013).

2.3 Increase in Industrial Conflict

The immediate result of this deliberate political choice to transform public services, including the opening-up of provision to competing private companies, was an enormous fragmentation of the areas affected and a splintering of established collective bargaining arrangements (see Dribbusch/Schulten 2007; Brandt/Schulten 2008). One consequence was a significant rise in the potential scope for industrial conflict as a small number of often national-level collective agreements and procedures were replaced by a plethora of branch-level agreements and hundreds of company agreements. Moreover, many of the new service providers were outside the scope of collective bargaining altogether, initiating a general trend in which branch-level agreements steadily forfeited their effectiveness (see Bispinck/Schulten 2009). Established collective arrangements were also eroded by an upsurge of restructuring in manufacturing operations in many established industrial firms, with routines previously performed in-house being outsourced to external firms (Helfen et al. 2016), leading to the emergence of a new service sector branch: contract logistics and contract manufacturing.

These processes were accompanied by a much greater readiness to engage in conflict on the part of firms and employer associations, to some degree accelerated by intensified competition and pressures to raise margins and profits. One consequence was that companies either withdrew from collective agreements or refused to negotiate at all. The most prominent instance of this in Germany is the dispute at Amazon which began in 2013 and was still unresolved in late 2018 (Boewe/Schulten 2015; Apicella 2016).

At the same time, German trade unions in the service sector also became more combative (Renneberg 2005). The unions' traditional reluctance to engage in strike action came under pressure when confronted with demands to cut into established negotiated terms and conditions from both private and public employers, leaving precious little space for constructive negotiations on improvements. The willingness of employees to make concessions, accept low pay and tolerate the lack of any financial recognition for their increasing workloads also declined, with an active core of trade unionists calling for organised resistance. Moreover, as seen at Amazon, no trade union can accept a flat refusal to engage. Some fresh impetus was also provided by a move to more adversarial Anglo-Saxon style campaigning and recruitment drives. Instead of fatalistically accepting declining memberships, there was a growing awareness that weak local workplace organisation and a lack of capacity to take industrial action were not unalterable fates (see, for example, Wohland 1998; Dribbusch 2003; Bremme et al. 2007; Kocsis et al. 2013).

For trade unions and union officials schooled in dealing with public sector work, as had previously been the case, adapting to these changes was not always easy. The erosion of collective bargaining was initially met by concessions in the hope that this would hold off further encroachments. Any form of confrontation or conflict was shunned, especially in the public sector. As late as 2015, interviews conducted by the present author following the four-week strike at Deutsche Post DHL – the longest strike ever in the postal service (Dörre et al. 2016, pp. 154–158) – indicated that some older trade unionists who had been "socialised" within the state-owned Bundespost were just as incensed about management's express decision to withdraw from the established practice of social partnership as they were about the hiving-off of the parcels service that had prompted the strike. Few had any experience of industrial action as the last major strikes at the Federal Postal Service had been back in 1990 and 1980.

By 2015, such a lack of experience had become rather untypical in the service sector. In 2005, for example, the demand by public sector employers in the Federal State of Baden-Württemberg to extend working hours signalled a turning point in employment relations that had been responded to by the services trade union ver.di with the longest strike ever held in the public sector (ver.di Landesbezirk Baden-Württemberg 2006). And also, in 2005, under pressure from junior doctors, the leadership of the doctors' trade union and professional body, the Marburger Bund (MB), embarked on an independent and militant negotiating strategy that involved withdrawal from the main public sector collective agreement and the pursuit of a separate agreement for doctors (Martens 2007). In the following year, the strike organised by MB to support this claim culminated in the final breaking of the taboo on holding industrial action in hospitals that had prevailed for far longer in Germany than elsewhere.

One consequence of the privatisation of health services was that the sector became the arena for a series of local "house-to-house" skirmishes, with industrial action at local level either to maintain collective bargaining or establish it. In 2007, the federal railway company (meanwhile, after the privatisation, under the name of Deutsche Bahn) experienced serious strikes for the first time in its post-war history when train drivers organised in the footplate trade union GDL also went on strike to secure their own collective agreement. The wider debate about growing inequality and the undervaluing of "female occupations" formed the context for a growing mobilisation by women in social and childcare services for proper recognition of their work, which, although acknowledged socially, was not commensurately rewarded (Kutlu 2013, 2015). The intensifying series of strikes by teachers, especially female teachers, organised in the education trade union GEW *(Gewerkschaft Erziehung und Wissenschaft)* since the mid-2000s are the direct consequence of a policy under which many teachers will not advance beyond the status of ordinary employees, putting them in a much worse position in terms of employment security and, in particular, pay when compared with colleagues granted the status of *Beamte*. And in the retail sector which has undergone a huge transformation in recent years (see Goes/Schulten 2016) it was the success of the campaign at the Schlecker drugstore chain (Wohland 1998) that promoted a new militancy, culminating in strikes in 2013 extending over several days, albeit not at national level. One consequence of all these developments was that a new generation of full-time union officials began not simply to "manage" sectors that had been previously regarded as a "challenge" but to develop new collective bargaining strategies with their memberships in these branches (Bremme et al. 2007; ver.di NRW 2014).

3 The Quantitative Picture

3.1 Preliminary Remarks: Strike Statistics in Germany

Strike statistics are often flawed and Germany is no exception (Dribbusch/Vandaele 2016). Official data on strikes and lockouts is collected by the Federal Employment Agency *(Bundesagentur für Arbeit, BA)*. Employers are obliged to inform the BA about the beginning and end of any strike or lockout. Although the frequency of strikes or lockouts is not recorded, there is a record of the number of establishments affected, the workers involved, and the number of days not worked. The main problem with the official data is that they under-record strike activity, mainly because employers do not always notify the BA of stoppages they have experienced (Dribbusch 2007; 2018). In 2008, the WSI (Institute of Economic and Social Research) set out to remedy these shortcomings and has established a new time series.

The series is an informed estimate based on data collected from trade unions and information in media reports (Dribbusch 2018). The WSI series starts in 2004 and is updated each year. Admittedly, the WSI estimate does not capture every instance of industrial action. Brief unofficial stoppages at workplace level, e. g., are usually neither recorded by unions nor will they come to the attention of the WSI through media reporting. Moreover, the WSI estimate depends on the different methods of counting used by the unions which may lead to under- or overestimations in particular cases: The union ver.di, for example, requires that all industrial action be officially approved by the ver.di executive committee and for many years the annual tally of such approvals was taken as a proxy for the number of disputes (ver.di 2014, p. 179). However, in 2015 an internal assessment (ver.di Fachbereich 03 2015) revealed that not all approved stoppages actually took place. In some cases, agreement might already have been reached by the time industrial action was approved; in others, it seems that local bargaining units had pre-emptively sought permission to strike in order to have the option ready if required. ver.di now estimates that at least a third of all approved actions do not materialise but precise figures are not available for all years.[3]

As a consequence, in 2015 the WSI initiated its own assessment of strike activity based on comprehensive web-based media research. The difficulty that presumably not all instances of industrial action become public can be mitigated in this way, although it cannot be eliminated.

The quantitative information in this section is based on WSI data if not indicated otherwise. The basic statistic, the number of days not worked due to industrial action (DNW), is a theoretical value that brings together the aggregate number of strike days reported by trade unions (that is, the total number of calendar days for which individual trade union members have received strike pay) and the WSI's own estimate of the days accounted for by warning (token) strikes for which unions do not provide strike pay. As with the official statistics, employees involved in strike action at different times or who participate in warning strikes might be counted several times. This occurs especially when there are large-scale waves of warning strikes. As a consequence, the number of employees involved in strike action can be much higher than the true number of individuals who have actually been on strike, either once or several times, in any given year.

---

3   The situation at IG Metall is the converse. In 2015, web-based research by the WSI found that the number of token strikes not registered by IG Metall was much higher than previously thought. Previous estimates of the trend of disputes (Bewernitz/Dribbusch 2014) were therefore revised by the WSI in 2017, also drawing on a similar and parallel study conducted at Jena University (Schneidemesser/Kilroy 2016).

3.2 The Development of Industrial Disputes since 1949

In order to put developments since the mid-2000s in context, it is worth looking at the incidence of strike activity in the preceding period. For the years between 1949 and 1980 we have fairly comprehensive data on strikes and lockouts collected by Spode et al. (1992). Then there is a big break in the statistics and data on strike frequency only became available again for the period from the mid-2000s when the WSI estimate stepped in (see *figure 1*). Up until 1980 it was the decade of the 1970s that displayed the highest strike frequency, with an average of 153 disputes involving strikes or lockouts each year. Although we have no data for the 1980s and 1990s there are good grounds to assume that the frequency of industrial action declined in this period. This makes it all the more remarkable that the number of industrial disputes involving stoppages ran at an annual average of 185 in the period from 2006 to 2017, thereby topping the 1970s.

The increase in the number of disputes, however, went along with a significant decline of days not worked due to industrial action (DNW) (see *figure 2*). The decline of DNW can largely be attributed to the fact that protracted industry-wide strikes have become less frequent, that there have no large-scale lockouts since 1984. The increase in the number of disputes since the mid-2000s has mainly been due to a rise in the incidence of smaller disputes in the context of single-employer bargaining which increased in accordance with the fragmentation of collective bargaining after the 1990s.

The tertiarisation of industrial conflict is visible in the increase of industrial disputes since the mid-2000s *(figure 1)*. Between 1949 and 1980 only 275 out of 2700 strikes identified by Spode et al. took place in the service sector; to this added 70 strikes in printing and publishing. Since the mid-2000s this picture changed. The tertiarisation is also evident when we look at the long-term development of the share of the service sector in the total number of DNW *(figure 3)*.

The service sector, which was largely absent in the strike statistics in the 1960s, showed a first sign of militancy in 1974 when the first national strike in the public sector took place. Since then the service sector has increasingly become the locus of industrial action although manufacturing remained dominant up to the mid-2000s. Then the picture completely turned around when an important increase in strike volume in the service sector coincided with the absence of large-scale strike action in manufacturing.

3.3 Strike Volume and Strike Participation in the Service Sector

There is enormous variation in the level and duration of employee participation in strike action, making it impossible to draw inferences about trends in either of these variables from any sheer increase in the number of industrial disputes (see *figure 4*). There was a peak in the number of days not worked due to strike action in 2006 and 2015, both of which were the result of two major disputes in each of those years. In 2006, this was the strike by local authority staff in Baden-Württemberg (noted above), which was prompted by the employer's demand for working hours to be extended, together with the large-

FIGURE 1

Annual number of disputes involving strike or lockouts, 1949–1980 and 2006–2017

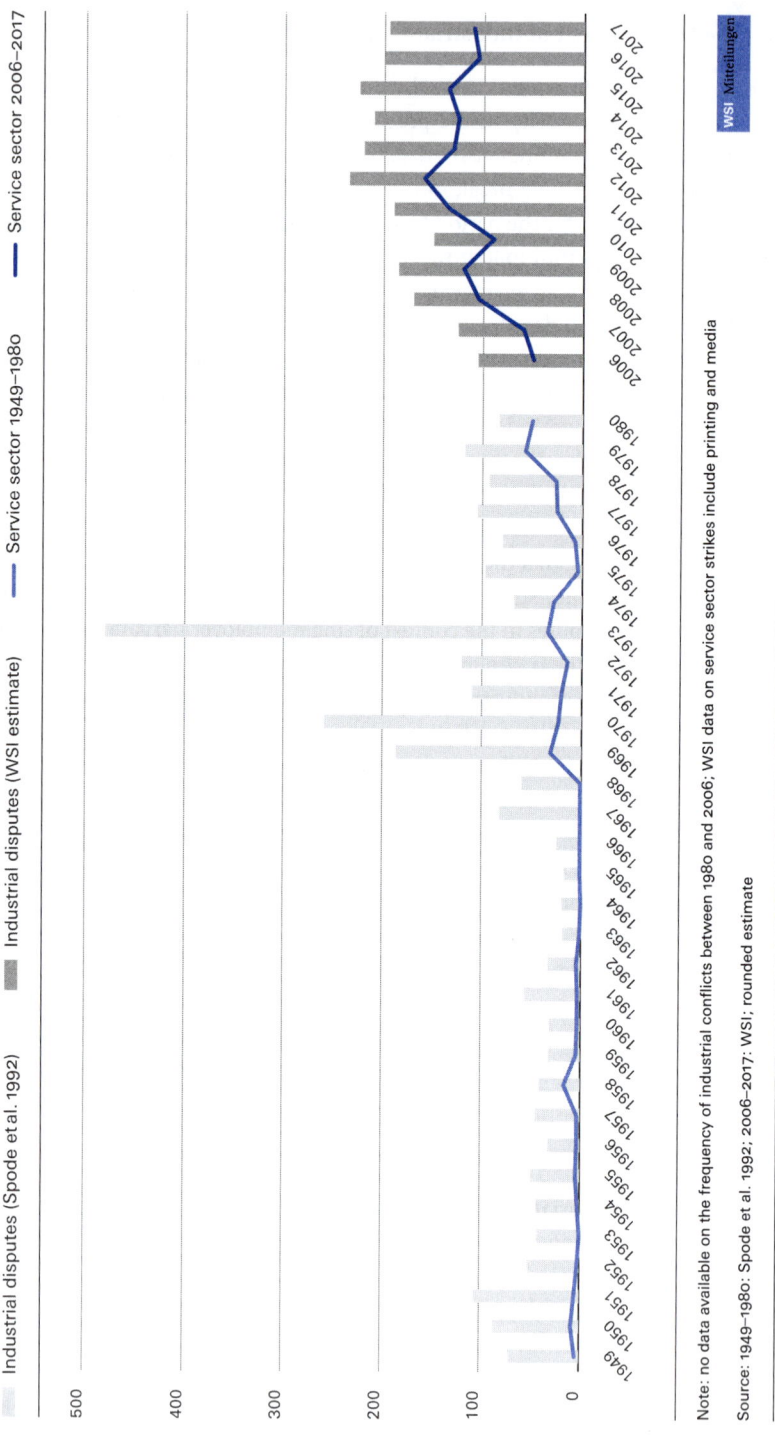

Industrial disputes (Spode et al. 1992)   Industrial disputes (WSI estimate)   Service sector 1949–1980 ——   Service sector 2006–2017 ——

Note: no data available on the frequency of industrial conflicts between 1980 and 2006; WSI data on service sector strikes include printing and media

Source: 1949–1980: Spode et al. 1992; 2006–2017: WSI; rounded estimate

FIGURE 2

Days not worked per 1000 employees (strikes and lockouts), 1950–2017, official record and corrected data

5-year averages (2015–2017: 3-year average)

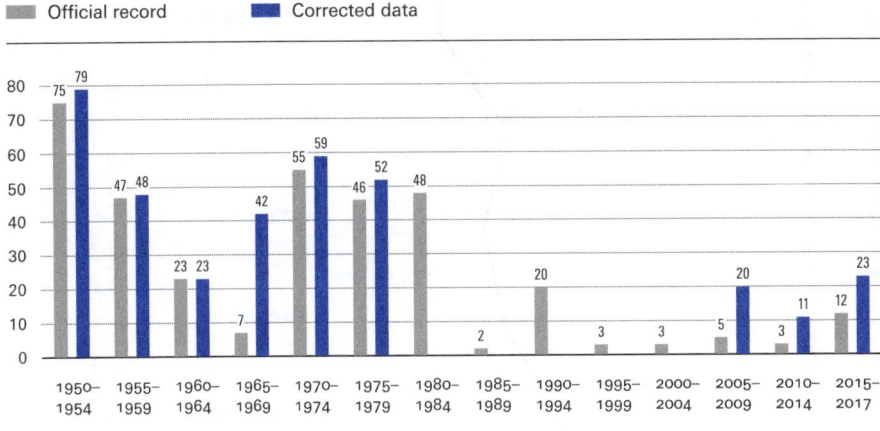

Source: Official record: Federal Employment Agency; corrected data: Spode et al. 1992 (1950–1980); WSI (2005–2017); own calculation

FIGURE 3

Share of service sector in total number of days not worked due to industrial action since 1960

Percentage shares of total

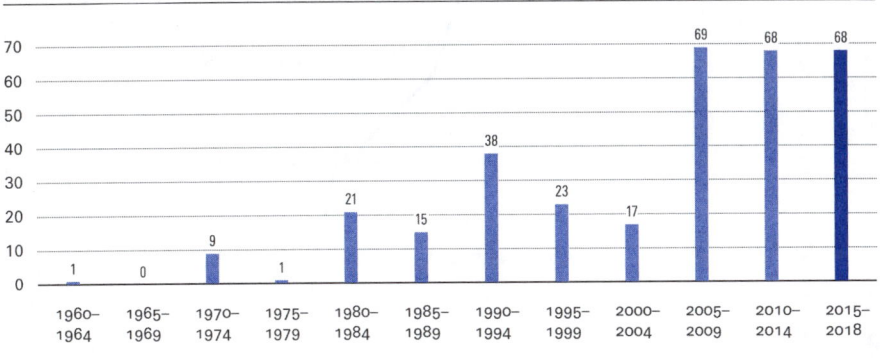

Source: Federal Employment Agency; own calculation

FIGURE 4

Number of industrial disputes, workers involved and days not worked (DNW) in the service sector, 2005–2017

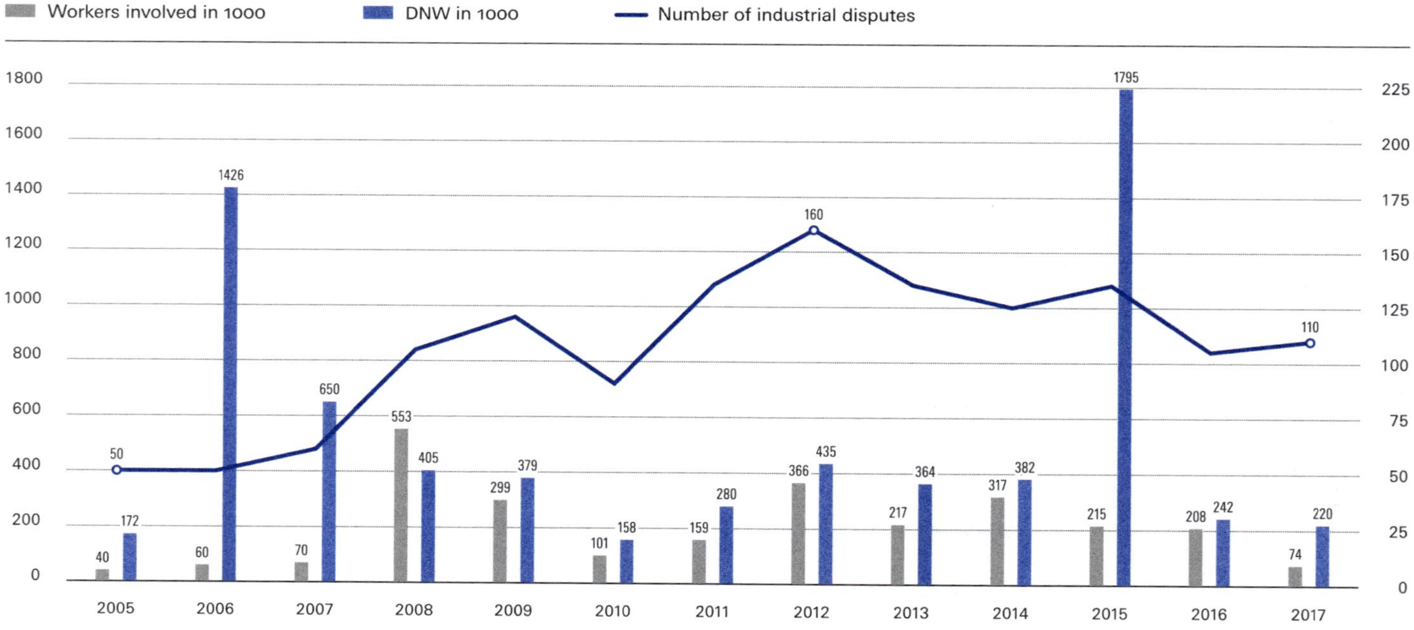

Workers involved in 1000 ▮ DNW in 1000 — Number of industrial disputes

Year	Workers involved in 1000	DNW in 1000	Number of industrial disputes
2005	172	40	50
2006	1426	60	—
2007	650	70	—
2008	405	553	—
2009	379	299	—
2010	158	101	—
2011	280	159	—
2012	435	366	160
2013	364	217	—
2014	382	317	—
2015	1795	215	—
2016	220	208 / 242	—
2017	220	74	110

Note: This diagram covers all strike activity by unions active in the service sector. This does not correspond exactly with the service sector as ver.di, for example, also organises in some areas of manufacturing, such as parts of paper processing, for which data cannot always be separately identified. Conversely, some manufacturing unions also organise in the service sector as for example in contract logistics.

Source: WSI Collective Bargaining Archive

scale dispute by the Marburger Bund for a separate collective agreement for hospital doctors. And in 2015, 1.5 million of the 1.8 million days not worked in the service sector were due to the disputes in social services and childcare and at Deutsche Post DHL. The peaks in strike activity in both years were the result of an unintended coincidence of separate disputes, not the expression of a mutually reinforcing, let alone coordinated, strike wave. This was especially so in 2015. As well as the two strikes referred to, there were notable disputes at Deutsche Bahn and the major German airline Lufthansa; both had begun in the previous year and dragged on into 2015 due to the hard line taken by management. In 2016 and 2017, the number of days not worked fell markedly as there were no large-scale disputes.

Small but high-profile strikes, such as that held by security staff at airports in North Rhine-Westphalia in 2013 (ver.di NRW 2014), the exemplary – in the true sense of the term – action at Charité in Berlin, and the numerous strikes by cabin and cockpit crews in aviation barely register in the official statistics.

Although the overall figures for industrial action indicate that in years with warning strikes in metal manufacturing the majority of strikers continue to be employees in industry, there has been a marked shift towards the service sector with regard to overall strike volume measured in terms of days not worked (see *figure 5*).

FIGURE 5

Days not worked and workers involved: annual share of service sector

Percentage shares

▨ Service sector: share of days not worked   ■ Service sector: share of workers involved

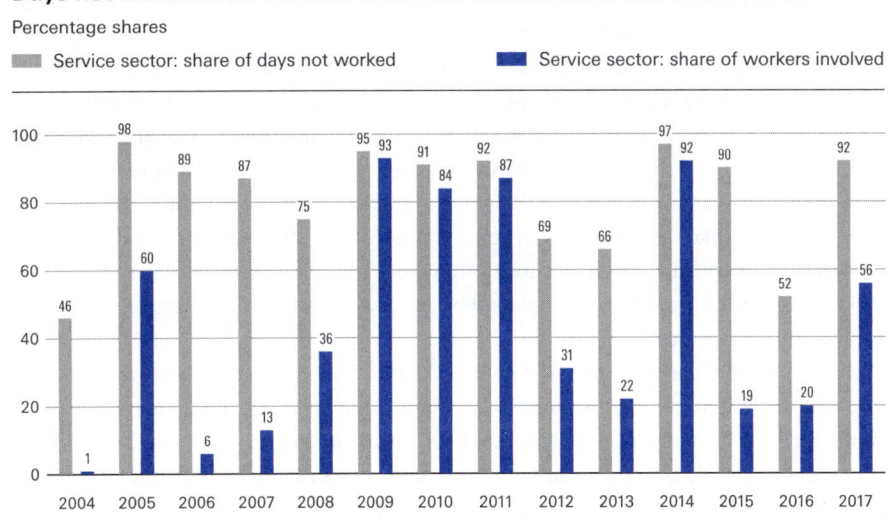

This new dominance on the part of the service sector should not be surprising given the absence of large-scale disputes in the metalworking and electrical industries in the years after 2003. One significant factor behind this is that the combination of full order books and highly-integrated manufacturing processes renders employers acutely vulnerable to the pressure exerted by extended token strikes. In 2015, the national confederation of metalworking employers' associations *(Gesamtmetall)* referred for example to "an unjustifiable and excessive volume of token strikes". Token strikes have a comparable effect only in a few sub-sectors, such as ground staff at airports who were included in the token action in the public sector in 2016.

3.4 Aspects of Gender and Branches

Strike statistics do not differentiate strikers by gender. It would be reasonable to assume that in years with large-scale strike action in the metalworking and electrical industries, most recently in 2018 when IG Metall mobilised more than a million strikers, the majority of participants were men. The picture is different in those major service sector branches that are notable for a high proportion of female employees, such as retail, social work and care, or health. The composition of employment is different in the postal services, public transport and local utilities, however. There are also no overall figures for strike participation by gender in the service sector. However, an analysis of the recipients of strike pay paid out by ver.di between 2005 and 2017 indicates that, based on the gender composition of employment in bargaining regions and workplaces that engaged in strike action, women were in a majority in 2009 and 2015 (strikes in social and care services) and in a narrow majority in 2013 and 2017 (strikes in retail) (see *figure 6*).

In fact, women were often central in determining the course of strike action. In retail, social and childcare services, commercial cleaning or teaching women accounted for up to three-quarters of strike participants and were the dominant force at strike meetings and at demonstrations. Analysing the gender aspect of industrial action is at a fairly early stage in Germany. Artus and Pflüger (2015) have offered some initial thoughts.

Large-scale token strikes are a regular feature of negotiations in federal and local government as well as in local authority transport and other services, where these still exist. These sectors have now been joined by social and childcare services together with local authority hospitals.

In terms of the sheer number of disputes, the most significant areas are private health and charitable welfare organisations. More than a quarter of all applications for approval for strike action at ver.di between 2008 and 2016 were in this division. Transport is also a focus of strike action and, as with the two previous examples, is characterised by a high degree of fragmentation of collective bargaining arrangements. Retail has been an enduring element in the strike statistics over the years. The driving force in this instance has been the employer associations; since the mid-1990s, these have combined a very restrictive approach to pay with a constant stream of new demands to amend existing agreed terms and conditions on such issues as supplements for evening working and

FIGURE 6

Annual recipients of ver.di strike pay: share of women and men

Percentage shares

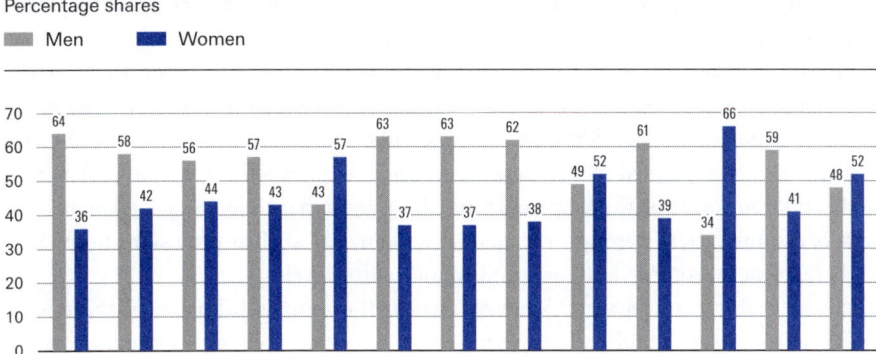

Source: ver.di; own calculation

WSI Mitteilungen

grading procedures. Strikes are also a regular occurrence in the media. Finally, regional governments at *Land* level, especially in eastern Germany, have made schools a focus of strike action through their decision to stop assigning public civil servant status *(Beamtenstatus)* to teachers: This represents an entirely novel situation, also for the trade union in this area, the GEW.

Hospitals, together with rail transport and aviation, are also areas in which occupational and sectional trade unions have become active. However, measured in terms of the number of disputes, employee participation in strike action and the actual number of days on strike – rather than public perception – these organisations are not disproportionately strike-prone (Bispinck 2015). Finally, the journalists' trade union DJV is frequently engaged in strike action, invariably organised jointly with another journalists' trade union, the dju *(Deutsche Journalistinnen und Journalisten Union),* which is part of ver.di.

3.5 Aspects of Motivation and Demands

Most strikes in the German service sector take place at company or workplace level and are directed at concluding agreements at this level. Employment terms and conditions in many organisations that deliver public services, but which are not formally within the scope of one of the public sector national-level collective agreements, are often set by "house" agreements that are broadly aligned with the appropriate national agreement. In some cases, there is an understanding that a local agreement will directly apply any national-level provisions that have been made. In many instances, therefore, local disputes occur parallel with the broader rhythm of the various collective bargaining rounds in the public sector, where there are separate negotiations for federal and local government, for regional *(Land)* government, and for some sub-sectors within these, and turn on securing the same outcome as the national negotiations.

The main issue prompting strike action is pay, which accounted for some 80 % of disputes in 2013, according to an analysis of applications for approval submitted to ver.di. In 40 % of these cases, in addition to pay, the indicated reason was other agreed provisions, typically enshrined in "framework agreements" and often affecting basic terms and conditions (such as working hours, holidays, and other time-off arrangements). In 10 % of disputes, there were specific qualitative demands, such as provisions for phased early retirement *(Altersteilzeit)* and minimum staffing levels.

Some strikes turn on very elemental issues. The most well-known of these were the disputes in social and childcare services in 2009 and 2015, where the aim was to improve basic material conditions for an area of work, mostly undertaken by women, that – although socially acknowledged – was poorly recognised financially in terms of how these jobs were graded (Kerber-Clasen 2017; Ideler 2017). Strikes by airport security staff in 2013 and 2014 were mainly prompted by a desire to end low pay in the sector. The 2015 strike at the Berlin hospital Charité was significant in this context as it was the first time that a claim had expressly addressed staffing levels and that relieving work-based stress was the core demand of an industrial dispute (Jäger 2015). This dispute turned on a central concern for nursing staff, creating a new awareness of the issue of unsustainable and unreasonable workloads and encouraging nurses elsewhere to contemplate similar action.

The strikes organised by Vereinigung Cockpit, the Marburger Bund, and the train drivers' union GDL were all aimed at securing separate bargaining arrangements for these groups of employees outside the main sectoral agreement typically negotiated by a DGB-affiliated union (often the multi-branch union ver.di). For its part, ver.di itself has been engaged in a protracted and as yet unresolved dispute with Amazon triggered by the refusal of the company to enter into collective bargaining with the union. There is no form of statutory procedure for trade union recognition in Germany and each union which has at least one member in a given establishment has the legal right to access the premises. However, employers are not obliged to agree to a collective agreement. If a union is not able to mount substantial industrial action, disputes about the establishment of collective bargaining tend to drag on for months, if not years.

There are also many instances of sympathy action intended to offer solidarity and support to those engaged in disputes at other workplaces in the same group of companies or branch.[4] Between 2011 and 2015, ver.di's executive committee approved 50 such actions.

---

4   In a court decision handed down on 19 June 2007, the Federal Labour Court *(Bundesarbeitsgericht)* substantially eased the previous restrictions on this form of strike action.

4 Capacity to Strike and Strike Effectiveness

The basic prerequisites for conducting a successful dispute are a capacity to mobilise for, and engage in, strike action combined with the effectiveness of the tactics used (Renneberg 2011, pp. 218f.). The capacity to mobilise and engage in a strike constitutes the central and autonomous source of power of trade unions. Considered abstractly, this is influenced by two main factors, subject to the specific institutional context involved (Silver 2003, p. 13). Firstly, it is based on structural power, which can be a function both of favourable economic circumstances or whether the employees involved occupy key roles in production or administration. And secondly, it rests on organisational ("associational") power in the form of the level of union membership and a union's capacity to mobilise its members. Employee willingness to strike is also therefore a further key factor. Where these preconditions are present, and to a sufficient degree, the mere threat of a strike can sometimes be sufficient to induce employers to settle.

This is not an automatic process, however, as the protracted dispute over pensions between Vereinigung Cockpit and Lufthansa which began in 2014 showed. Although the striking pilots were well organised and could not be replaced at short notice, literally occupying the driving seat in civil aviation, they ran into a brick wall in the shape of a management that was both well-prepared and obdurate. Despite repeated stoppages by the pilots the dispute dragged on for several years before being settled by a compromise in which the union had to make substantial concessions in March 2017.

Nonetheless, staff in key positions can more easily put pressure on employers than those for whom a strike would either have no immediate impact or who could easily be replaced. The 2013 strike by airport security staff in North Rhine-Westphalia, part of a wider dispute in the security industry, was noteworthy in this respect (ver.di NRW 2014). The fact that this walkout proved highly effective led to a far better outcome for other security staff with less scope to exert pressure. As a consequence, the employers in the private security industry split the employers' association in 2017 with the aim of taking the airport security out of the industry-wide collective agreement and thus preventing further joint bargaining for airport and ordinary security staff. The new national employers' association for airport security staff insisted then on national bargaining. This move, however, fired back. It offered ver.di the opportunity to demand the long overdue harmonisation of wages for security staff at east and west German airports. When this was rejected the union successfully mobilised for a national strike movement in January 2019 which finally secured disproportionately high wage increases for east German staff resulting in the full harmonisation of wages by 2021.

4.1 Union Presence in the Service Sector

As far as organisational power is concerned, the service sector is problematic in several respects. Aside from a small number of union strongholds, trade unions are often only weakly anchored in many service branches. The dispersion of employees in many small workplaces that is typical of much of the service sector not only hampers trade union organisation (Dribbusch 2003), but also makes organising strike action a logistical challenge. Simply conducting employee surveys and ballots requires enormous time and expense where a workforce is geographically scattered, as was the case with staff at childcare facilities.

Organisational power is both the precondition for, but also an outcome of, industrial action. Any trade union that wants to mount an effective response to an employer provocation will need to master the difficult art of conducting a successful strike from a minority position (Riexinger 2013). And if successful, such a strike can serve as a jumping-off point for further organisational consolidation. Such a strategy of "organising through conflict" (detailed in Dribbusch 2011, 2016) can be an organising catalyst where there is already an engaged workplace trade union presence (see also Birke 2010, p. 83). However, this requires several preconditions to be met and is not an approach that can be implemented in all circumstances.

For strikes to function as a catalyst for effective workplace organising, they must either be successful or address an issue with a mobilising potential. The most striking example is the rise in membership in municipal social and childcare services since the mid-2000s. The strike in the public sector in the *Land* of Baden-Württemberg in 2006 had a first positive impact and the national disputes of 2009 and 2015 boosted membership levels substantially (see *figure 7*). The fact that Baden-Württemberg shows a more positive development than the national level is related to the elevated level of union activity in this region. In particular both the 2009 and 2015 disputes in eastern Germany had a much smaller scope than those in western Germany. In talks with the author, eastern German union officials attributed the comparatively low strike level in eastern Germany at least partly to the fact that while childcare employees in Baden-Württemberg compare their wages and conditions to those in the automotive industry their east German colleagues consider their job in public childcare to be comparatively secure and well-paid employment.

Much more difficult is the picture in retail, one of the biggest industries in private services and the theatre of repeated bargaining disputes since the late mid-1990s. What is striking in retail is that since the mid-2000s, despite repeated disputes involving virtually thousands of stoppages, membership levels have been in decline. The only exception to this was a temporary spike in the context of the 2013 bargaining dispute. The employers triggered a wave of entries into the union when they demanded the termination of the collectively-agreed supplements for unsocial hours.[5] But although the union managed to secure these provisions at the end of a months-long dispute the fall in mem-

---

5　The entries were largely motivated by the interest of employees to be securely covered by the umbrella of the framework collective agreement for the retail industry. Provisions of collective agreements in Germany are legal norms which retain "subsequent validity" *(Nachwirkung)* unless a new agreement is concluded. However, this legal provision only applies to those

FIGURE 7

ver.di membership development in social services and childcare, national level and Baden-Württemberg, 2005–2017

Indexed (2005 = 100)

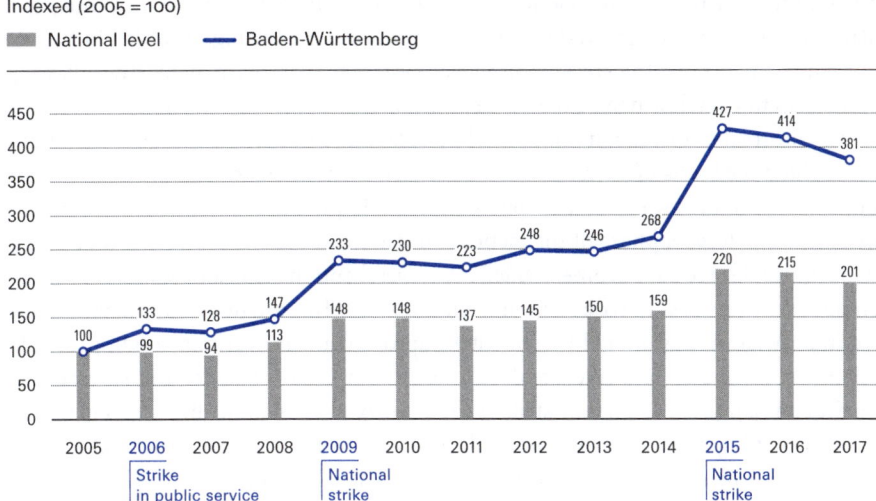

Source: ver.di; own calculation

bership resumed the following year. One part of the explanation for the membership decline is that the union was severely hit by the insolvency of a number of well-union-ised firms in the sector (such as the drugstore chain Schlecker, the DIY chain Prakti-ker and others). However, an equally important reason is that ver.di does not have the capacities to follow the structural changes in the industry (Dribbusch 2003). While the traditional department store was comparatively well organised, the union always had trouble organising across thousands of outlets belonging to the emerging food discount chains. The capacity of ver.di to stage effective industrial action has much developed since the late 1990s but it has done so in a comparatively small number of strongholds. The regional organisation of ver.di in Baden-Württemberg – one of the most strike-prone in the industry – considers there to be a structural weakness of the union in the sector with a membership density of less than 10 % and a capacity to strike in a one-digit percentage of retail establishments (ver.di Landesbezirk Baden-Württemberg Fachbe-

employees who are members of the concluding union at the point in time when the agreement expires without being replaced by a new one.

reich Handel 2018, p. 48). It is not only a minority of employees in the industry that go on strike, it is also only a small minority of employers who are hit by industrial action.

Some hope comes from examples like the fashion chain H&M. Not only did many employees participate in repeated strike action in the 2013 dispute, but they also developed a range of novel strike tactics (Fütterer/Rhein 2015). Engagement in industrial action was preceded by innovative and member-based organising, in which initiatives to set up works councils were supported by a system of workplace mentoring, allowing employees to gain first-hand experience in dealing with workplace conflict.

The protracted dispute at Amazon (Boewe/Schulten 2015) on the other hand has highlighted the limits of striking from a minority position. Following the failure of the initial wave of strikes in 2013, despite considerable public and political support, the dispute has entered a phase of the tactics of attrition; at many of the company's operations the workforce has become divided into several entrenched camps, with one group emphatically opposed to strike action (Apicella 2016). This might be due, in part, to the fact that Amazon has offered incremental improvements in working conditions, a development attributed by strikers and the trade union to the sustained pressure exerted on the company, but which non-strikers see as an expression of the firm's goodwill. The strikers' best hope is that at some point the company will agree on a settlement in order to end the permanent irritation of continuing industrial action.

An interesting case is the health sector, by far ver.di's main growth area. While most new members have not joined as a result of a strike (ver.di Fachbereich 03 2015), the union has raised its profile as a representative of employees' interests by way of some exemplary struggles such as the campaign against overwork and stress at Charité. The union has also developed an organising strategy called "condition-based bargaining" (Dilcher 2011). It is an approach that recognises that certain preconditions must exist at workplace level for the effective conduct of negotiations, first and foremost being a certain level of trade union organisation, backed up by a high degree of identification between employees and the union, and the perception that the claim is a legitimate one.

4.2 The Effectiveness of Strike Action

The usual measure of the effectiveness of a strike is the economic pressure produced by a withdrawal of labour. This is at its highest where strikes remain solid and the employer side is unable to sidestep or avoid the consequences. One exemplary instance of this took place on 21 February 2014, when baggage security staff at Frankfurt airport went on strike without prior warning. The scale of the mobilisation involved surprised even their own trade union, ver.di. Baggage clearance came to a rapid standstill and the one-day stoppage secured a 25 % pay rise over two years for the security staff who, despite not being seen as part of the airport elite, demonstrably possessed an enormous potential for disruption (HBS 2015).

Strikes are also particularly effective along highly-integrated and sensitive supply chains, especially those based on just-in-time deliveries. Even small-scale stoppages at significant suppliers can have far-reaching effects. However, such configurations are rather exceptional and in many disputes the balance of forces between employers and strikers is not as clear and the effect of any individual stoppage much less calculable.

Strikes in the public sector are subject to a set of specific circumstances. Given that public services are not generally provided on the basis of immediate payment through fees or charges, the financial impact of stoppages on public employers is limited or can even be positive. Such strikes achieve their desired effect through the exercise of political pressure. A major role in this is played by the overall political situation and whether trade unions can forge coalitions between strikers and the users of public services.

Strikes outside the public sector can also affect third parties. Typically, these will be other firms, and the pressure these might put on those employers who are subject to strike action can be helpful for employees in a dispute. However, where strikes affect the wider public, both strikers and their trade unions need to develop a capacity for building alliances and constructing an appropriate narrative (see Kutlu 2013; Kerber-Clasen 2017). The construction workers' union IG BAU *(Industriegewerkschaft Bauen-Agrar-Umwelt)* was successful in this during its strike for a minimum wage in the commercial cleaning industry in 2009 (see Birke 2010, pp. 161–166). This dispute, in which strikers embarked on industrial action from a fairly weak position, was met with wide public sympathy that considerably strengthened their hand. There was also some public understanding for the train drivers' strike despite the intense media campaign against their union, the GDL (Ecke 2015).

Creating an informal alliance between strikers and those affected by strike action can be especially challenging where, as in the 2015 strike by childcare staff, the affected parties – in this case parents – had to manage the immediate consequences. In this instance, it was not possible to set up alternative forms of childcare to help alleviate the loss of care as the strike became more protracted (Birke 2017). This enabled local authorities, which saved money by not having to pay for subsidised childcare, to sit out the strike until pressure from many parents turned against the strikers. This problem first became apparent in 2009. Despite the long run-up period, neither ver.di nor GEW were able to organise an effective response during the second strike in 2015.

4.3 Influencing Factors and Conditions for Success

Strike costs: As a rule, strikers in Germany are also trade union members. One important factor in this is access to strike pay, which is a core benefit of union membership and is also paid by several unions in the service sector in the event of token strike action. At ver.di, for example, strike pay is due after four hours of a token stoppage.[6] What

---

6   The monthly contribution is 1% of monthly gross pay. Members with more than twelve months' membership will receive two-and-a-half times their monthly union subscription for each eight hours for which they have lost earnings, plus a small child supplement. So, a worker with

striking employees individually lose in net terms will depend on how long a strike lasts and their tax band. Long strikes by low-paid workers with limited financial resources will inevitably create difficulties for them.

Trade unions also have to manage the financial consequences of strike action, and the opinion of union treasurers will come to play an increasingly important role during protracted and large-scale disputes. In September 2015 alone, ver.di spent more than € 100 million on strikes (ver.di 2015, p. 87). This is a serious number, despite a high level of income from union dues (€ 454 million in 2015) and the fact that 8 % of dues had been paid into the union's strike fund since 2012, with access to reserves if needed (ver.di 2014, p. 196). As a consequence ver.di has become more restrictive in its approach to approving industrial action, with encouragement to adopt new tactics involving fewer strike days and less cost. This does not, however, mean that it has given up on militancy. During the 2018 national bargaining round in federal and local government, ver.di successfully mobilised several hundred thousand employees, winning substantial increases in pay. Strike action was highly selective, with the aim of winning public attention and support. The union's success was helped by the generally tight labour market, which convinced the employers they had to take steps to raise the attractiveness of the public sector.

Strike tactics: Industrial action has changed in Germany in recent years (Dribbusch 2009) and this also applies to the service sector. Instead of large-scale "unlimited" industry-level strikes, in which employees remain on strike until a settlement is reached, industrial action now takes the form of token strikes of up to a day, organised on a rolling basis in which workplaces take it in turns to strike. Prolonged disputes will consist of a series of linked but separate strike days. Rolling one-day strikes have proved an effective form for mobilising employees with little experience of industrial action. At the same time, this limits the impact on third parties and helps retain public sympathy.

How effective this tactic can be was put to the test in 2008 during a strike in the retail branch. The strike, involving some 6500 individual and scattered one-day stoppages, had begun in 2007 but had started to flag after a year without a settlement. It was only after resorting to targeted prolonged action in the Baden-Württemberg region that a result was obtained (see ver.di Baden-Württemberg Fachbereich Handel 2009). As a result, in 2013 the ver.di regional branch in Baden-Württemberg, which was the first to bargain in the branch that year, opted for several days of strike action from the outset. However, the fact that the action was relatively limited meant that this did not markedly shorten the dispute.[7] Eventually, and after eight months, the larger retailers in the regional em-

---

monthly earnings of € 1500 should pay monthly dues of € 15 and would receive a strike pay of € 37.50 per eight hours of lost earnings. Strike pay is not taxable.

7   According to ver.di's figures, 950 retail establishments were affected by a strike in 2013; given that Baden-Württemberg has some 38 000 retail outlets in the food sector, 1800 self-service supermarkets and around 200 department stores, this is a very small proportion (source for data: WABE Institut, Berlin).

ployers' association felt that the risk of a strike at Christmas was too great, leading to a compromise settlement that was generally accepted by the strikers (Kobel 2014).

In 2015, ver.di decided to draw the lesson from its experience in the 2009 dispute in social and childcare services and abandon the tactic of short stoppages, which had led to repeated conflicts with parents, and move straight to a national unlimited strike in a "breakthrough strategy", without any prior general discussion within the union as to what escalation or exit strategies would be available should the employers refuse to concede and sit out the strike, which is, in fact, what took place.

In the dispute at the Berlin hospital Charité, a strike tactic tailored to the specific circumstances of a medical facility was developed after several years of preparation and extensive discussion (Jäger 2015). The challenge remains as to how this might be implemented more widely (Windisch 2017). As of 2018, ver.di has managed to engage a few other hospitals in similar disputes. In addition, the union has been pressing for legislation to address the problem of understaffing in hospitals.

Membership participation: Not all strikes are the same. There is a difference, for example, between a short token strike by local authority transport workers with extensive experience of industrial action that involves leaving their vehicles in the depot for a few hours and a first-time strike by a small group of workers at a branch of a fast-food outlet who switch off the kitchen equipment at lunchtime and leave for a strike meeting. The decision to stop work in a service establishment often calls for a considerable degree of courage and represents the most important step in a dispute. Beyond this, however, strikers also need to get involved in other activities to back up their industrial action and gain public attention. And finally, there has to be scope for involvement and discussion to ensure that the strike can remain resilient in the face of external pressure. The strategy of "organising through conflict" is, therefore, closely bound up with the development of mobilising approaches to industrial action, as tried in several instances since the mid-2000s (see Riexinger 2013; Seppelt 2014). One important element in this is the strike meeting; this can be an important mechanism for tackling employee isolation, especially where a workforce is widely geographically dispersed. During the strikes in social and childcare services in 2009 and 2015, ver.di organised national meetings of strike delegates to review the course of the dispute. And in October 2009, ver.di amended its internal industrial action procedure to allow for membership surveys to be used in decision making, in addition to the existing requirements for formal strike ballots. Under the new provision, ver.di's national executive committee can arrange for a survey to be conducted during a dispute once a settlement has been proposed: Should more than 75 % of the respondents reject the proposal, the executive can decide to continue with the industrial action.

Strikes are more likely to be conducted effectively where members are included and mobilised, which presupposes and requires effective and plentiful communication. This poses an organisational challenge to trade unions, however, as decision-making will become more complex and strikers will often be critical of any negotiated settlement, as seen in the rejection of the initial mediation settlement in the social services and childcare strike in 2015. That these forms of member participation are not used in all circumstances was evident in the strike at Deutsche Post, which took place at the same time (see Teuscher 2015). For tactical reasons, not only was the strike begun without a prior ballot, but ver.di's negotiating committee also decided to accept the proposed settlement without consulting members, prompting considerable unease and criticism on the part of strike activists. This dispute was also complicated by the fact that, for legal reasons, the strike was only nominally about shortening working hours: The real main demand was to bring the parcels delivery business back within the scope of the main company agreement. And it was on this fundamental issue that the company had refused to move.

Duration and outcome: Many disputes turn out to be very lengthy. Notable examples include the dispute at Amazon, which began in 2013, and the protracted conflict between Lufthansa and Vereinigung Cockpit. A large number of disputes with hospital operators lasted for several months, as did strikes in the retail bargaining round. There is, however, no linear relationship between the length of a strike and its success or otherwise. Protracted strikes often reflect the lack of options for escalation on the part of the trade union or a deadlock between the parties.

The question as to the point at which a strike might be regarded as successful is only rarely amenable to an objective answer. Strikes are only rarely abandoned without any kind of outcome; alternatively, strikers do not usually win all their demands. Most disputes end with mixed results. The crucial point is how the strikers themselves perceive the final compromise. This is not solely a matter of the relationship between demands and outcome but also reflects the course of the strike and individuals' assessment of the power relationships at play.

5 Future Prospects: the Long Haul

Strikes are not an end in themselves. According to a 2007 DGB survey, almost 90 % of employees thought it was important for unions to be able to conclude negotiated settlements without a strike (DGB 2007). Depending on the balance of forces involved, this reflects the desire, under normal circumstances, to be able to influence the employer side by alluding to the "sword on the wall". The various experiments and search processes that have characterised the more combative recent disputes in the service sector might be seen as efforts to create the preconditions for such an approach. In other words, striking today could mean having to strike less in the future. To continue the metaphor: For the sword to be fastened securely, but threateningly, on the wall, it first has to be forged.

In 1992, around one-third of employees in Germany were members of a trade union; by 2017, this had fallen to around a sixth, with even lower figures in some areas of the service sector. This has consequences. At present, trade unions can only mount effective industrial action in a small number of service branches. Recent developments suggest that this situation is not simply being accepted as a given. Strikes have taken place in areas where such action was formerly seen as inconceivable. A new generation of employees has started to look at the poor conditions they work in as something that can be changed. In particular, younger full-time trade union officials have begun to redefine their work, drawing inspiration less from established bargaining rituals than from the examples of the militant forms of action developed by social movements. This is not a linear process. Setbacks occur and need to be reflected on and dealt with; and not every instance of success can be reproduced elsewhere. Nonetheless, there is a fresh readiness to risk trying something new.

Nachtwey (2016) has offered the metaphor of an escalator running backwards to denote the situation in which many, but not all, employees now find themselves. Anyone who isn't already at the top needs to struggle against the direction of the mechanism to avoid slipping downwards. From this perspective, strikes in the service sector can be viewed as attempts to stop the movement and, if possible, reverse its direction.

REFERENCES

Accornero, A. (1985): La 'terziarizzazione' del conflitto e i suoi effetti, in: Cella G. P. / Regini, M. (eds.): Il conflitto industriale in Italia, Bologna, pp. 275–313

Apicella, S. (2016): Amazon in Leipzig. Von den Gründen, (nicht) zu streiken, https://www.rosalux. de/publication/42258/amazon-in-leipzig.html [accessed 21 March 2017]

Artus, I. (2017): Das „ungewöhnlich intensive" Streikjahr 2015. Ursachen, Ergebnisse, Perspektiven, in: Prokla (186), pp. 145–165

Artus, I. / Pflüger, J. (2015): Feminisierung von Arbeitskonflikten. Überlegungen zur gendersensiblen Analyse von Streiks, in: AIS-Studien 8 (2), pp. 92–108

Bewernitz, T. / Dribbusch, H. (2014): „Kein Tag ohne Streik". Arbeitskampfentwicklung im Dienstleistungssektor, in: WSI-Mitteilungen 67 (5), pp. 393–401

Birke, P. (2010): Die große Wut und die kleinen Schritte. Gewerkschaftliches Organizing zwischen Protest und Projekt, Berlin/Hamburg

Birke, P. (2016): Die Entdeckung des „labor unrest", http://www.soziopolis.de/erinnern/klassiker/ar tikel/die-entdeckung-des-labor-unrest [accessed 18 December 2018]

Birke, P. (2017): Schwierige Solidarität. Eltern, Kinder, Erzieher_innen im Streik 2015, in: Artus, I. / Birke, P. / Kerber-Clasen, S. / Menz, W. (eds.): Sorge-Kämpfe. Auseinandersetzungen um Arbeit in sozialen Dienstleistungen, Hamburg, pp. 90–113

Bispinck, R. (2015): Wirklich alles Gold, was glänzt? Zur Rolle der Berufs- und Spartengewerkschaften in der Tarifpolitik, http://gegenblende.dgb.de/++co++ebcfc60c-f7b6-11e4-bce0-52540066f352 [accessed 18 December 2018]

Bispinck, R. / Schulten, T. (2009): Re-Stabilisierung des deutschen Flächentarifvertragssystems, in: WSI-Mitteilungen 62 (4), pp. 201–209

Boewe, J. / Schulten, J. (2015): Der lange Kampf der Amazon-Beschäftigen. Labor des Widerstands: Gewerkschaftliche Organisierung beim Weltmarktführer des Onlinehandels, https://www. rosalux.de/publication/41916/der-lange-kampf-der-amazon-beschaeftigen.html [accessed 21 March 2017]

Böhlke, N. (ed.) (2009): Privatisierung von Krankenhäusern: Erfahrungen und Perspektiven aus Sicht der Beschäftigten, Hamburg

Bordogna, L. / Cella, P. G. (2002): Decline or transformation? Change in industrial conflict and its challenges, in: Transfer 8 (4), pp. 585–607

Brandt, T. / Schulten, T. (2008): Liberalisierung und Privatisierung öffentlicher Dienstleistungen und die Erosion des Flächentarifvertrags, in: WSI-Mitteilungen 61 (10), pp. 570–576

Bremme, P. / Fürniß, U. / Meinecke, U. (eds) (2007): Never work alone. Organizing – ein Zukunftsmodell für Gewerkschaften, Hamburg

Brookes, M. (2018): Power resources in theory and practice. Where to go from here, in: Global Labour Journal 9 (2), pp. 254–257

DGB (Deutscher Gewerkschaftsbund) (2007): DGB Potenzialstudie. Ergebnisse einer repräsentativen Erhebung. TNS Infratest, not published

Dilcher, O. (2011): Handbuch bedingungsgebundene Tarifarbeit, https://gesundheit-soziales.verdi.de/++file++588a5df824ac062de5645107/download/ver.di-Handbuch-Tarifarbeit.pdf [accessed 18 December 2018]

Dörre, K. / Goes, T. / Schmalz, S. / Thiel, M. (2016): Streikrepublik Deutschland? Die Erneuerung der Gewerkschaften in Ost und West, Frankfurt a. M. / New York

Dribbusch, H. (2003): Gewerkschaftliche Mitgliedergewinnung im Dienstleistungssektor. Ein Drei-Länder-Vergleich im Einzelhandel, Berlin

Dribbusch, H. (2007): Industrial action in a low-strike country. Strikes in Germany 1968–2005, in: van der Velden, S. / Dribbusch, H. / Lyddon, D. / Vandaele, K. (eds.): Strikes around the world 1968–2005. Case-studies of 15 countries, Amsterdam, pp. 267–297

Dribbusch, H. (2009): Streik-Bewegungen, in: Forschungsjournal Neue Soziale Bewegungen 22 (4), pp. 56–66

Dribbusch, H. (2011): Organisieren am Konflikt. Zum Verhältnis von Streik und Mitgliederentwicklung, in: Haipeter, T. / Dörre, K. (eds.): Gewerkschaftliche Modernisierung, Wiesbaden, pp. 231–263

Dribbusch, H. (2016): Organizing through conflict: exploring the relationship between strikes and union membership in Germany, in: Transfer. European Review of Labour and Research, 22 (3), pp. 347–365.

Dribbusch, H. (2018): Arbeitskampfbilanz 2017. Deutlicher Rückgang der Ausfalltage trotz anhaltend vieler Konflikte, Wirtschafts- und Sozialwissenschaftliches Institut: Policy Brief (22), https://www.boeckler.de/pdf/p_wsi_pb_22_2018.pdf [accessed 29 September 2018]

Dribbusch, H. / Schulten, T. (2007): The end of an era: Structural changes in German public sector collective bargaining, in: Leisink, P. / Steijn, B. / Veersma, U. (eds.): Industrial relations in the new Europe. Enlargement, integration and reform, Cheltenham, pp. 155–176

Dribbusch, H. / Vandaele, K. (2007): Comprehending divergence in strike activity. Employers offensives, government interventions and union responses, in: van der Velden, S. / Dribbusch, H. / Lyddon, D. / Vandaele, K. (eds): Strikes around the world, 1968–2005. Case-studies of 15 countries, Amsterdam, pp. 366–381

Dribbusch, H. / Vandaele, K. (2016): Comparing official strike data in Europe – dealing with varieties of strike recording, in: Transfer. European Review of Labour and Research 22 (3), pp. 413–418

Ecke, O. (2015): Agenda-Setting 2.0: Die neue Öffentlichkeit, Vortrag, Medientage 2015, Munich

Fütterer, M. / Rhein, M. (2015): Erneuerung geht von unten aus. Neue gewerkschaftliche Organisierungsansätze im Einzelhandel. Das Beispiel H&M, https://www.rosalux.de/fileadmin/rls_uploads/pdfs/Analysen/Analysen21_H_M.pdf [accessed 18 December 2018]

Gesamtmetall (2015): Wir hatten nicht zu rechtfertigende Warnstreikexzesse, https://www.gesamtmetall.de/aktuell/interviews/wir-hatten-nicht-zu-rechtfertigende-warnstreikexzesse [accessed 18 December 2018]

Goes, T. E. / Schulten, J. (2016): Ausweitung der Kampfzonen. Monopolisierung und Prekarisierung im deutschen Einzelhandel, in: Z. Zeitschrift marxistische Erneuerung 27 (108), pp. 101–115

HBS (Hans-Böckler-Stiftung) (2015): WSI Arbeitskampfbilanz 2014, https://www.boeckler.de/wsi-tarifarchiv_52621.htm [accessed 18 December 2018]

Hedemann, U. / Worm, L. / Artus, I. (2017): „Mehr von uns ist besser für alle". Dokumentation einer Veranstaltung zum Pflegestreik an der Charité, in: Artus, I. / Birke, P. / Kerber-Clasen, S. / Menz, W. (eds.): Sorge-Kämpfe. Auseinandersetzungen um Arbeit in sozialen Dienstleistungen, Hamburg, pp. 116–129

Helfen, M. / Nicklich, M. / Sydow, J. (2016): Interorganisationale Netzwerke und tarifpolitische Fragmentierung. Hebt Mehr-Arbeitgeber-Beschäftigung die Tarifeinheit aus den Angeln?, in: Industrielle Beziehungen 23 (3), pp. 280–308

Ideler, K. (2017): Aufwertung reloaded. Die Tarifauseinandersetzung im Sozial- und Erziehungsdienst 2015 aus gewerkschafts- und geschlechterpolitischer Sicht, in: Artus, I. / Birke, P. / Kerber-Clasen, S. / Menz, W. (eds.): Sorge-Kämpfe. Auseinandersetzungen um Arbeit in sozialen Dienstleistungen, Hamburg, pp. 76–89

Jäger, M. (2015): TV MGM Charité, presentation at the WSI-Tariftagung, held on 17 October 2015 in Düsseldorf, http://www.boeckler.de/pdf/v_2015_10_07_jaeger.pdf [accessed 18 December 2018]

Kädtler, J. (2013): Tarifpolitik und tarifpolitisches System, in: Schroeder, W. (ed.): Handbuch Gewerkschaften in Deutschland. 2nd., revised ed., Wiesbaden, pp. 425–464

Keller, B. (1993): Arbeitspolitik des öffentlichen Sektors, Baden-Baden

Kerber-Clasen, S. (2017): Erfolgreich gescheitert? Gewerkschaftliche Aushandlungen des Sozialstaatsumbaus im Kita-Bereich, in: Artus, I. / Birke, P. / Kerber-Clasen, S. / Menz, W. (eds.): Sorge-Kämpfe. Auseinandersetzungen um Arbeit in sozialen Dienstleistungen, Hamburg, pp. 34–57

Kobel, A. (ed.) (2014): Wir sind stolz auf unsere Kraft. Der lange und phantasievolle Kampf um die Tarifverträge 2013 im Einzelhandel, Hamburg

Koscis, A. / Sterkel, G. / Wiedemuth, J. (eds) (2013): Organisieren am Konflikt. Tarifauseinandersetzungen und Mitgliederentwicklung im Dienstleistungssektor, Hamburg

Kutlu, Y. (2013): Partizipative Streikführung: Der Erzieherinnenstreik, in: Schmalz, S. / Dörre, K. (eds.): Comeback der Gewerkschaften? Machtressourcen, innovative Praktiken, internationale Perspektiven, Frankfurt a. M. / New York, pp. 226–241

Kutlu, Y. (2015): Kampf um Anerkennung. Die Sozial- und Erziehungsdienste im Streik, in: Z. Zeitschrift marxistische Erneuerung 26 (103), pp. 126–140

Lesch, H. (2015): Strukturwandel des Arbeitskampfs. Deutschland im OECD-Ländervergleich, in: IW Trends 42 (3), pp. 1–21

Martens, H. (2007): Primäre Arbeitspolitik und neue Gewerkschaft? Der Ärztestreik im Frühjahr und Sommer 2006, in: Jahrbuch für Kritische Medizin (44), Hamburg, pp. 120–137

Müller-Jentsch, W. (1997): Soziologie der Industriellen Beziehungen. Eine Einführung, Frankfurt a. M. / New York

Nachtwey, O. (2016): Die Abstiegsgesellschaft. Über das Aufbegehren in der regressiven Moderne, Berlin

Renneberg, P. (2005): Die Arbeitskämpfe von morgen? Arbeitsbedingungen und Konflikte im Dienstleistungsbereich, Hamburg

Renneberg, P. (2011): Arbeitsbuch Tarifpolitik und Arbeitskampf. Theorie und Praxis gewerkschaftlicher Tarifarbeit und betrieblicher Arbeitskämpfe, Hamburg

Riexinger, B. (2013): Demokratisierung von Streiks. Revitalisierung der Gewerkschaftsarbeit, Presentation at the conference Erneuerung durch Streik, 1–3 March 2013 held in Stuttgart, Berlin

Schmalz, S. / Dörre, K. (2014): Der Machtressourcenansatz. Ein Instrument zur Analyse gewerkschaftlichen Handlungsvermögens, in: Industrielle Beziehungen 21 (3), pp. 217–237

Schneidemesser, L. / Kilroy, J. (2016): Der Streikmonitor, in: Z. Zeitschrift marxistische Erneuerung 27 (106), pp. 160–171

Seppelt, J. (2014): Demokratisierung als Schlüssel für den Aufbau von Organisationsmacht: Erfahrungen des ver.di Bezirks Stuttgart, in: WSI-Mitteilungen 67 (5), pp. 402–405

Silver, B. (2003): Forces of labor, Cambridge, MA

Spode, H. / Volkmann, H. / Morsch, G. / Hudemann, R. (1992): Statistik der Arbeitskämpfe in Deutschland: Deutsches Reich 1936/37, Westzonen und Berlin 1945–1948, Bundesrepublik Deutschland 1949–1980, St. Katharinen

Teuscher, S. (2015): Tarifkonflikt bei der Deutschen Post AG: eine Tarifauseinandersetzung um Schutz und Sicherheit! Presentation at the WSI-Tariftagung, held on 17 October 2015 in Düsseldorf, https://www.boeckler.de/pdf/v_2015_10_08_teuscher.pdf [accessed 18 December 2018]

ver.di (2014): Geschäftsbericht 2011–2014: Stärke. Vielfalt. Zukunft, Berlin

ver.di (2015): 4. Bundeskongress, Leipzig 2015, Tagesprotokoll 21. September

ver.di Baden-Württemberg Fachbereich Handel (2009): Neue Streikbewegung im Handel. 15 Monate Tarifrunde im baden-württembergischen Einzelhandel 2007/2008, Stuttgart

ver.di Baden-Württemberg Fachbereich Handel (2018): Geschäftsbericht 2015–2018, Stuttgart

ver.di Fachbereich 03 (2015): Statistikauswertung der Arbeitskampfmaßnahmen im ver.di-Fachbereich 03 der Jahre 2011–2014, unpublished evaluation

ver.di Landesbezirk Baden-Württemberg (ed.) (2006): Unser Streik 2006. Streikdokumentation Landesbezirk Baden-Württemberg, Stuttgart

ver.di NRW (ed.) (2014): Auch unsere Löhne sollen abheben. Bilanz des Arbeitskampfs im Wach- und Sicherheitsgewerbe in Nordrhein-Westfalen und Hamburg 2013, Düsseldorf

Windisch, W. (2017): „Wir haben es selbst in der Hand, noch stärker zu werden!" Die Bewegung für einen Tarifvertrag Entlastung in den saarländischen Krankenhäusern, in: Artus, I. / Birke, P. / Kerber-Clasen, S. / Menz, W. (eds.): Sorge-Kämpfe. Auseinandersetzungen um Arbeit in sozialen Dienstleistungen, Hamburg, pp. 130–153

Wohland, U. (1998): Die Schlecker Kampagne, in: Alternative 10 (98), pp. 7–9

AUTHOR

HEINER DRIBBUSCH, Dr. rer. pol., is Senior Researcher at the Institute of Economic and Social Research (WSI) within the Hans-Böckler-Foundation in Düsseldorf, Germany. His field of research covers industrial relations with a special focus on trade unionism, collective bargaining and industrial conflicts.

 E-Mail: Heiner-Dribbusch@boeckler.de

The Impact of the Jurisprudence of the Court of Justice of the European Union on Germany's Collective Bargaining System

How is the German model of industrial relations affected by European integration, particularly by the case law of the Court of Justice of the European Union (CJEU)? What are the effects on the autonomy of collective bargaining? The analysis of selected rulings shows that the impact of the Court's jurisprudence is ambivalent. In the area of individual labour law, the rights of workers have been strengthened. In contrast, in the area of collective labour law, the Court has restricted the autonomy of collective bargaining. [1]

DANIEL SEIKEL, NADINE ABSENGER

1 Introduction

European integration affects the collective bargaining systems of the member states of the European Union (EU) in a wide variety of ways. Measures in response to the euro crisis (economic governance, Troika) allow the EU to directly influence national collective bargaining systems and wages: Under pressure of the Troika – composed of

1   This article is a translation of the German article „Die Auswirkungen der EuGH-Rechtsprechung auf das Tarifvertragssystem in Deutschland", published 2015 in: Industrielle Beziehungen 22 (1), pp. 51–71. Please note that, therefore, the article presents the legal situation prior to 2015. Recent developments such as in the area of posted workers (see section 4.3) like the CJEU decision *Sähköalojen ammattiliitto ry v Elektrobudowa Spółka Akcyjna* (C-396/13) in 2015 or the revision of the Posted Workers Directive in 2018 are not covered. Some of these later developments have partially reversed the juridical trends we observed in the original article, as did the *Asklepios* case (C-680/15, C-681/15) in 2017 with regard to the applicability of collective agreements after transfers of business undertakings (see section 4.4). The translation was provided by Yvonne Marchand. We thank Martin Behrens, Martin Höpner, Thorsten Schulten, and two anonymous reviewers of the journal "Industrielle Beziehungen" for their valuable advice. Parts of the empirical data used here were collected in association with project A6 of the Collaborative Research Center 597 "Transformations of the State" of the University of Bremen, which was financed by the German Research Foundation DFG.

the European Central Bank (ECB), the European Commission, and the International-al Monetary Fund (IMF) –, member states had to lower wages in the public service sector, reduce minimum wage levels, and decentralise collective bargaining systems (Fischer-Lescano 2014; Schulten/Müller 2013). These massive intrusions have led to intensive public disputes and to governments being voted out of office.

Another point that in comparison has received far less public attention – at least outside the law community – is the impact that the decisions of the Court of Justice of the European Union have on collective labour law. These decisions have been affecting the scope of the actions of the collective bargaining parties for a much longer time already and have been doing so not only in the crisis countries but in such highly coordinated economies as Sweden and Germany as well.

The fact that supranational institutions are restricting the freedom of collective bargaining, including the right to strike or wage issues, is rather astonishing considering that European primary law explicitly excludes wages, the right of association, and the right to strike from the unions' competences. If the freedom of collective bargaining is understood as a guarantee of the decision-making prerogatives of the collective bargaining parties – and therefore of the autonomy of the democratic decisions of collective organisations (Kocher 2010, p. 482) –, then the restriction, in some cases massive restriction, of the discretionary powers of the bargaining parties by the CJEU can hardly be justified.[2]

At least since the judgments of the CJEU in *Laval* (C-341/05), *Viking* (C-438/05), *Rüffert* (C-346/06), and *Commission v Luxembourg* (C-319/06) it has become clear that the judicial decisions of the CJEU have a major impact on the national industrial relations systems of the member states. Although the CJEU in *Viking* and *Laval* held that the right to strike is a fundamental right (Kocher 2009, p. 163), it afforded higher priority to economic freedoms using an unusually strict test of proportionality based on a rather questionable review of strike goals. In Sweden, the *Laval* judgment led to a substantial restriction of the right of Swedish trade unions to strike. Swedish trade unions may no longer use industrial actions to force foreign service providers to conclude collective agreements (see Seikel 2014). Woolfson et al. (2010) are of the opinion that the Swedish model has been fundamentally altered. Does this European judge-made law have a similar impact on the industrial relations system in Germany? Based on selected rulings that are particularly relevant to industrial relations, this article analyses from a political science and law perspective the impact that the jurisprudence of the CJEU has on the collective bargaining system and on the autonomy of the collective bargaining parties in Germany.

---

2   We understand the freedom of collective bargaining in a technical sense as the regulatory autonomy of employers and trade unions to regulate certain aspects of the economic sphere by means of collectively binding agreements.

The case law of the CJEU is a double-edged sword; in the area of *individual* labour law, the decisions of the Court often favour the rights of employees. This strengthens the individual rights of employees, for example with respect to their rights in relation to temporary employment contracts and working time.[3] Yet, the decisions on individual labour law are in no way always advantageous to employees, especially when provisions of collectively negotiated agreements are involved. At least in those cases in which the CJEU holds that a provision of a collective agreement is incompatible with European law, e. g. on account of unlawfully discriminating on the basis of age, as it did for example in *Prigge* (C-447/09, see section 4.1), employees might lose collectively bargained entitlements that for many years were regarded as socially adequate. In the area of *collective* labour law (e. g. the right to strike), however, the decisions are often detrimental to employee rights and trade unions. This is particularly problematic in systems in which collective bargaining parties – such as in Germany – have a large degree of regulatory autonomy. Höpner and Schäfer (2010) observe a convergence towards a market-liberal model legally administered by the CJEU. Does this hypothesis hold true for German industrial relations?

From a political science perspective, two observations appear particularly relevant: First, the interaction between legislated minimum requirements and judicial decisions can result in an unintended decline in social standards – for example in the area of posted workers following the *Laval* and *Rüffert* decisions. Second, the ability to correct politically the CJEU-driven legal development of the fundamental freedoms appears limited.[4]

This article is structured as follows: Following the introduction in section 1, section 2 summarises the current state of industrial relations research into the impact of the European integration process on national industrial relations systems. Section 3 provides an overview of the main features of the development of European case law. Section 4 uses selected examples to investigate how the decisions of the CJEU impact Germany's collective bargaining system. Section 5 summarises and discusses the findings.

---

3   One example is the *Kücük* decision (C-586/10): The CJEU determined that when judging whether a successive chain of temporary employment contracts is justifiable, the total number and the duration of such temporary contracts concluded with the same employer must be taken into account. Up to then, the German Federal Labour Court had only taken the last temporary contract into account. In the *Jaeger* decision (C-151/02) in 2005 the CJEU ruled in favour of employee protection that hours during which employees are on-call are working hours within the meaning of the German Working Hours Act (Arbeitszeitgesetz, ArbZG). In *Schultz-Hoff* (C-350/06) the CJEU ruled that the vacation entitlement of employees on long-term sick leave does not lapse upon the expiration of the statutory period pursuant to which unused vacation can be carried over to the next year in cases where such employees were unable to take vacation due to their incapacity for work.

4   This essentially confirms the findings of Scharpf (2010a) and Schmidt (2010).

2 European Integration and Industrial Relations

What does the literature on industrial relations say about the impact of the European integration process on national industrial relations systems in general and about the role of the decisions of the CJEU in particular? There is a well-established body of research into how the integration process impacts labour relations in the member states (see for example Behrens 2013, pp. 217ff.; Hyman 2001; Marginson 2006; Marginson/Sisson 2006; Streeck 1998, 2000; Teague 1999; Visser 2005; Vos 2006). However, the effect of the CJEU's jurisprudence has only attracted marginal attention up to now.

The EU is an independent regulatory level for the governance of industrial relations, even though no fully integrated European system of labour relations has yet evolved or is being strived for.[5] According to Teague (1999, p. 160), the EU is a crossbreed of member state autonomy and European regime, albeit one that does not lead to a convergence of national models (see also Marginson/Sisson 2006, p. 24f.; Streeck 1998, p. 429f.). A qualitative innovation in this respect is, however, the new system of economic governance introduced in the wake of the euro area crisis since 2010.

The industrial relations literature identifies five main factors relevant to national labour relations. First, the creation of the European Single Market intensified competition between national labour market regimes. This competition is often held responsible for a downward competitive deregulation spiral in relation to wages, working conditions, labour market regulations, and collective social rights (Marginson 2006, p. 98). It also provides companies and investors with additional opportunities to "decide with their feet" (exit option). Alone the threat of withdrawing capital, of refusing to invest, or of moving production facilities elsewhere provides capital givers with additional leverage in national political disputes (see also Keune 2008, pp. 298ff.; Streeck 1998). According to Streeck (1998, p. 438), these new "escape routes" turn what were formerly obligatory national institutions into voluntary institutions for employers.

Second, the Economic and Monetary Union (EMU) has a disciplinary effect on national wage negotiations, because the ECB, in compliance with its mandate, is forced to react to inflationary wage agreements with countercyclical increases in interest rates. In addition, the countries of the euro area can no longer adjust their exchange rates. In

---

5   A full harmonisation of the industrial relations systems is neither permitted under EU primary law nor is it desired by the member states (including employers and trade unions). The member states entrust – to different degrees – the regulation of labour conditions to autonomous collective negotiations, which come with various forms of labour dispute requirements and whose political-economic aims are widely different for historic-cultural reasons (Kocher 2009, p. 164). The institutional differences between these collective negotiating systems are also the main reason for the restrictions found in Article 153 (5) of the Treaty on the Functioning of the European Union (TFEU), which expressly excludes wages, the right of association, the right to strike, and the right to impose lockouts from the scope of EU competencies (ibid.).

case of macroeconomic imbalances between the euro area countries, national labour markets and wage policies have to bear the main burden of economic adjustment (Marginson/Sisson 2006, p. 6). Thereby, wage negotiations become the "main release valve" for regulating the pressures of international competition, and collective bargaining negotiations are subordinated to the imperatives of competition and job security (Grahl/Teague 2005; Keune 2008, pp. 300ff.; Marginson/Sisson 2006, p. 6; Schäfer/Streeck 2008, pp. 218f.). National labour relations take the nature of "competitive corporatism", and the decentralisation of collective bargaining systems is fostered (Marginson/Sisson 2006, p. 153; Rhodes 1998; Streeck 1998).

Third, the EU responded to the euro area crisis with far-reaching measures (Six Pack, Two Pack, Fiscal Compact, etc.). The new coordination of economic policy is used to put national wage-setting systems under pressure. Contrary to the restrictive provisions of Article 153 (5) TFEU, the structural adjustment programmes imposed on crisis countries aim at the convergence of national models towards a decentralised type of industrial relations. In countries receiving financial support, the Troika even orders direct wage reductions, privatisations, the lowering of minimum wages, the abolition of mechanisms for making collective agreements generally binding, and the weakening of national and sectoral collective bargaining negotiations to the advantage of the corporate level (on this, see Busch et al. 2013; Schulten/Müller 2013).

Fourth, regulatory measures that fall within the area of European social policy (Article 153 TFEU) have a direct effect on national regulations. Included here are not only labour law directives and regulations (see Behrens 2013, pp. 217ff.) but also "soft law" measures (non-compulsory requirements) such as the open method of coordination of national policies, and the social dialogue (for an overview, see Falkner et al. 2005; Keune 2008). Because of the high majority requirements (unanimous or qualified majority) in the EU and the large institutional and socio-economic heterogeneity of the member states (cf. Höpner 2013), governments often agree on the "smallest common denominator" only, i. e. on minimum standards or on regulations that preserve national autonomy as far as possible. Therefore, for many countries, European provisions – if they allow for higher standards – are often nothing more than mere supranational codifications of the national status quo (Keune 2008, p. 287; Streeck 1998; Teague 1999, p. 142).

The fifth factor is the case law of the CJEU. Despite the intensive treatment of European integration in the industrial relations literature, a systematic consideration of the role of the CJEU is seldom found in it, even if increased attention is paid to the decisions of the Court since the *Laval* case (see for example Dolvik/Visser 2009; Lillie/Greer 2007). This is astonishing considering how strongly the CJEU's decisions affect labour-market regulations and social policies in the member states. Moreover, it is also often unclear which role European integration actually plays in the transformation of national labour relations and which developments are attributable to other sources of change such as globalisation or deindustrialisation. In this article, we examine an area – i. e. the decisions of the CJEU – that without doubt is a relevant and independent supranational influence of its own.

3 Legal Developments in the EU Driven by Judge-Made Law

The development of European law has been shaped to a very large extent by principles of law and competencies created by judge-made law (Alter 2001; Weiler 1994). Although the ongoing development of European law is based on a continual cumulation of many single judgments, five central judicial "acts of creation" can be identified that have led to European law becoming an "effective instrument for economic liberalisation" (Höpner 2008, p. 12; translation: D. S./N. A.). This development was hardly foreseeable by the member states at the time the European Economic Community was founded in 1957. Already in the early stage of European integration, the CJEU made it clear in its 1962 decision *van Gend & Loos* (C-26/62) that certain parts of European primary law have a direct effect. In many cases, both primary and secondary law (on the latter: *van Duyn* C-41/74) apply not only to the member states themselves but are also binding on and legally enforceable by the citizens and private institutions of the member states. It was also in the early stages of integration that the European judges in *Costa/ENEL* (C-6/64) and in subsequent decisions postulated that European law fundamentally has priority over national law – including over national constitutional law (Weiler 1994, pp. 513ff.).

Another significant step was taken in *Dassonville* (C-8/74) and *Cassis-de-Dijon* (C-120/78). In these cases, the general prohibition of discrimination anchored in the European treaties – i. e. the prohibition to treat citizens from other EU countries in a manner inferior to nationals when importing or exporting goods and services – was reinterpreted as a general prohibition of restriction: The court held that any actual or potential restricting of inner-Community trade is incompatible with European law unless such restriction is justifiable by "mandatory requirements" of public order. The CJEU also created the principle of mutual recognition: Standards that are recognised as sufficient by one member state must also be accepted by the other member states and may not be used to block market-access (country of origin principle) (Höpner 2008, p. 153; Schmidt 2010, p. 460). In *Defrenne* (C-43/75) and *Walrave and Koch* (C-36/74), the CJEU held that some of the provisions of the EU treaties – especially the fundamental freedoms – apply to private entities such as federations and associations. The Court determined that the fundamental freedoms also apply to collective bargaining parties in that it regarded employer associations and trade unions as quasi-public law-makers (Kocher 2010, p. 479). The CJEU has extended these principles little by little from the free movement of goods to all other fundamental freedoms (services, persons, capital) (Schmidt 2010).

In the past, the CJEU has repeatedly subjected elements of national labour and social law, and also collective agreements, to reviews of compatibility with European law. In earlier times, however, these reviews had more the character of reviews of arbitrariness. The fundamental freedoms were not used to modify the basic elements of national labour law with a mind to harmonising them with other member state models. Up to the end of the 1990s, the position taken by the CJEU could be described as relatively autonomy-preserving. For example in *Albany* (C-67/96), the judges stated that the scope of the discretionary powers of collective bargaining parties may not be restricted by competition law. According to the *Albany* decision, collective agreements are not subject to competition law because EU law not only aims at protecting competition but also at recognising the pursuit of social policy goals. The CJEU argued that although collective agreements, by their very nature, involve restrictions of competition, the attainment of the social policy goals strived for with collective agreements is seriously imperilled if the provisions of European antitrust law were to apply to collective bargaining parties in their pursuit for measures to improve employment and working conditions (on this, see Kingreen 2014, pp. 19f.).

In recent years, however, the decisions of the CJEU have become increasingly more "radical" (Scharpf 2008). Meanwhile, it is the differences between the member states in the areas of labour law and industrial relations that attract the attention of the CJEU as potential obstacles to cross-border trade (Dolvik/Visser 2009, p. 494). The fundamental freedoms have become an instrument for reshaping national laws that were previously matters of national autonomy (Höpner 2008, p. 17). National social policies, and particularly collective protection rights of employees, both legislative or collectively agreed, often have to be justified because they are perceived as constraints on cross-border commercial activities; the economic freedom rights of business restrict the range of national market-correcting interventions (Kocher 2009, p. 165).[6]

The following examples illustrate in detail how the decisions of the CJEU affect the German system of industrial relations.

4 The Impact of the CJEU's jurisprudence on Germany's System of Industrial Relations

4.1 CJEU Jurisprudence on Anti-discrimination in Relation to Age-related Provisions of Collective Agreements

The area of anti-discrimination is a good example of the effect of the CJEU's jurisprudence on Germany's collective bargaining system, here particularly the prohibition against discrimination on the basis of age.[7] Both European law (Article 21 of the Charter of Fundamental Right of the European Union, Council Directive 2000/78/EC) and German law (Paragraphs 1 and 7 of the General Act on Equal Treatment, AGG) prohibit discrimination on the basis of age. However, it is discrimination that is prohibited and

---

6   This is also clearly seen in the CJEU decision in *Alemo-Herron* (C-426/11); see section 4.4.

7   On the CJEU decisions in the area of age discrimination, see Zeibig (2013a; 2013b).

not every act of unequal treatment on the basis of age. Unequal treatments are permitted, inter alia, if within the context of national law they are justified by a legitimate aim, especially from the areas of employment policy, labour market, and vocational training, and if they are appropriate and necessary (Article 6 of Council Directive 2000/78/EC, Paragraph 10 AGG). There are numerous collectively agreed provisions in Germany that hinge on age, for example wages based on age, vacation entitlements and termination notice periods scaled according to age, and special dismissal protection for older employees. Since the coming into force of the European Equal Treatment Directive (2000/78/EC) and the German AGG, however, a variety of age-based collectively agreed provisions, which for years had been in existence and regarded as socially adequate, have been held by the CJEU in recent years to be unlawful forms of discrimination on the basis of age.

Age-related pay scales: In *Hennigs/Mai* (C-297/10, C-298/10), for example, the CJEU ruled that the basic-wage groups of the Federal Collective Framework Agreement for Public Employees *(Bundesangestelltentarifvertrag, BAT),* who are scaled according to age, are incompatible with European law because they relied solely on age for calculating the basic wages. The Court was of the opinion that they constitute an unlawful discrimination of younger persons, because it is not age that may be used as the decisive factor for calculating the remuneration of occupational experience but rather seniority, if necessary in combination with age. The CJEU confirmed once again in this decision that the collective bargaining parties are bound by European law and by the Equal Treatment Directives. In the opinion of the CJEU, the fact that EU law stands in the way of a provision of a collective agreement does not interfere with the right anchored in Article 28 of the Charter of Fundamental Rights of the European Union (CFREU) to negotiate and conclude collective agreements. In general, social partners as well as member states are entitled to adopt measures at national level that involve the unequal treatment of persons based on age. Yet, when doing so, the right of collective bargaining anchored in Article 28 of the Charter must nevertheless be exercised in line with EU law. Therefore, the social partners must observe the prohibition of discrimination on the basis of age when enacting their regulations, in the opinion of the CJEU in *Hennigs.* The Court affirmed that although the collective bargaining parties have wide discretionary powers, every unequal treatment on the basis of age must be reasonable and necessary for attaining the pursued social policy goals. The consequence of this decision and the subsequent decision of the German Federal Labour Court *(Bundesarbeitsgericht, BAG)* (BAG 6 AZR 481/09) was that employees who had been discriminated against by the BAT wage provisions could demand repayment. In this case, they had a right to an "upwards adjustment" of their wages – a positive decision for the employees who had been disadvantaged up to then, but a costly affair for the employer side. It also meant that the relevant wage provisions had to be renegotiated.

Collectively-agreed age limit for the automatic termination of employment relationships: Another decision of the CJEU – the *Prigge* case (C-447/09) – also had significant consequences. In this case, the CJEU held that Lufthansa's collectively-negotiated compulsory retirement age of 60 years, after which pilots are not allowed to exercise their profession, was incompatible with EU law on account of its unlawful discrimination on the basis of age (subsequent decision of the German Federal Labour Court, BAG 7 AZR 904/08). Lufthansa took advantage of this judgment to cancel the collectively-negotiated transitional retirement-pension entitlement (for the period between 60 years and the statutory retirement age of 65 years, so-called *Übergangsversorgung*) of the Lufthansa pilots as per 31 December 2013. Lufthansa argued that because the pilots were now allowed to work until 65 years of age, the transitional retirement pension was no longer necessary. The pilots' trade union Cockpit objected to this, arguing that the transitional pension was crucial for the pilots because their entire career planning is based on it. Cockpit has initiated numerous industrial actions since 2014 to secure the transitional pension system but has been unable to date to achieve a preservation of the transitional retirement pension.

These examples clearly illustrate the double-edged nature of the CJEU decisions in the area of age-related discrimination. In relation to wage discrimination, the elimination of discrimination is a welcome development for employees who have been disadvantaged by it. But for trade unions and employer associations it means that collective agreements that were concluded prior to the enactment of the Equal Treatment Directive and that for many years had been regarded as appropriate and socially adequate now have to be negotiated anew and in a more restrictive framework. It is also a costly affair for employers who have to pay back wages. What the *Prigge* case also shows, however, is that CJEU decisions can be used by employers to challenge existing employee rights and to use them as bargaining chip, as happened with the transitional pensions of the pilots. Another problem with the decisions of the CJEU on age discrimination is that the decisions often go beyond the wording of Council Directive 2000/78/EC, which creates a great deal of uncertainty for the social partners when negotiating collective agreements. For example, the CJEU – unlike the wording of Council Directive 2000/78/EC – now only allows social policy goals from the areas of employment policy, labour market, and vocational training as justification for an age-related unequal treatment (C-447/09; C-159/10; C-388/07). Up to now, the German Federal Labour Court had also accepted other interests as justifications for unequal treatments of persons on the basis of age, for example for attaining a balanced age structure or for reasons of competition law (BAG 2 AZR 523/07). The restrictive interpretation of the CJEU narrows the wide discretionary powers explicitly afforded to the collective bargaining parties by the German Federal Labour Court on numerous occasions.

4.2 Compliance with European Procurement Law when Concluding Collective Agreements

Another case from the area of European procurement law serves as an example of how CJEU decisions affect the German system of collective bargaining and the social partners' autonomy. In an infringement proceeding against Germany (C-271/08), the CJEU reviewed the practices of municipal employers to award contracts for services in relation to company pension benefits to a specific, collectively negotiated circle of providers of such insurance services without Europe-wide tender procedure.[8] The CJEU dealt with the question of whether European procurement law applies to collective agreements and, accordingly, whether the corresponding services require a public tender. The Court affirmed these questions, holding that the procurement directives are a concretisation of the freedom to provide services and that the conflicting rights had to be balanced in an appropriate way. The judges stated that although the function of collective agreements was to reach a common solution while taking into account the respective interests of the collective bargaining parties in reaching their social policy goals, the requirements of public procurement law still had to be complied with. Only a few years before this, the CJEU had referred in *van der Woude* (C-222/98) to the *Albany* decision (C-67/96; see section 3) and held that the parties to collective agreements were free to make decisions regarding additional health insurance coverage for employees, including the choice of the insurer (Kingreen 2014, pp. 34f.).

Otherwise, the freedom of the social partners would be restricted in an unjustified manner. However, in *Commission v Germany* (C-271/08), the CJEU came to the opposite conclusion without explicitly abandoning its own former position. The Court treated collective agreements in relation to antitrust law *(Albany)* differently than in relation to the fundamental freedoms (Kocher 2010, p. 477) without explaining why in this case – unlike in the *Albany* case – the decision-making freedom afforded to the social partners should no longer apply in *Commission v Germany*. The special purpose of collective agreements, i. e. to achieve social policy goals, was basically no longer considered relevant here. The CJEU ruled that the collective agreement parties could readily have agreed on solutions that complied with EU law and with which the aspired social policy goals could equally have been achieved (ibid., p. 482). Although the *Albany* case involves a different legal area (antitrust law) than *Commission v Germany* (freedom to provide services), it is unclear why the social policy function of collective agreements should be taken into account in relation to antitrust law but not in relation to the fundamental freedoms, both being parts of EU primary law.

4.3 The Single Market Freedoms and the Regulation of the Working Conditions of Posted Workers[9]

Subordinating the right to strike to single market freedoms: The following judgments belong to a series of four CJEU decisions – the so-called *Laval* Quartet[10] – in which

---

8 For details on this, see Kingreen (2014, pp. 34f.) and Kocher (2010, pp. 476ff.).

9 Note that this article does not take the recent legislative revision of the Posted Workers Directive (2018) into account. The revision solved some of the problems the CJEU had caused with regard to the regulation of working conditions of posted workers. For example, it makes the full application of collective agreements to posted workers possible again – if the national legislator sets the necessary conditions (see Seikel 2018). However, the reform did not correct the imbalance

national measures to counteract wage competition practices were held to be unjustified infringements of the freedom to provide services or of the freedom of establishment.

The CJEU decisions in *Viking* (C-438/05) and *Laval* (C-341/905) resulted in a massive restriction of the right to strike. In the *Viking* case, a Finnish trade union wanted to prevent a Finnish ferry (operating between Finland and Estonia) from registering the vessel under a flag of another country. In the *Laval* case, a Swedish trade union wanted to use industrial actions to force a Latvian construction company operating in Sweden to conclude a Swedish collective agreement.

The test of proportionality applied by the CJEU in these cases ultimately resulted in a questionably strict review of the goals of strikes (Kocher 2010, p. 469). Such a rigorous scrutiny is foreign to many national legal systems, including the German. The CJEU demanded in the *Viking* case that the jobs affected by the registration under the flag of another country must be *de facto* threatened (to be proven by the trade union) in order to render a restriction of the single market freedoms lawful (Kempen 2010, pp. 33f.). It therefore obliged trade unions to observe general public interests although their actual purpose is to pursue their own economic and collective interests (Kocher 2010, p. 479), and virtually subordinated fundamental social rights, such as the right to strike, to the economic fundamental freedoms (here the freedom of establishment). The requirements stipulated by the CJEU for a lawful industrial action pose a considerable risk for trade unions due to the large sums of damage claims that they are threatened with. On this, Kempen (2010, p. 34) states that the burden of incalculable incorrect prognoses and lawsuits for damages reduces the historically hard-won fundamental right of association to a mere speculative chance of a fundamental right.

Although these two decisions have not yet had any direct impact on Germany, German trade unions are very much aware of them. Strikes by German trade unions in the case of offshoring activities could be affected in future as they may be seen as restrictions of the freedom of establishment. Industrial actions could also be affected when trade unions use strikes to achieve collectively negotiated social compensation plans to regulate the repercussions of company closures (ibid., p. 33f.).

Restriction of Tariftreue (wage loyalty): In the *Rüffert* case (C-346/06), the CJEU dealt with the State of Lower Saxony's act on public procurement. The so-called *Tariftreue* provisions obliged construction companies carrying out public contracts to pay at least the wages stipulated in local collective agreements. The CJEU ruled that the *Tariftreue* provision constituted an unjustifiable infringement of the freedom to provide services

---

created by the Court between the right to strike and the economic freedom rights of the single market. To date, a fundamental rebalancing of collective social rights and economic freedoms is still pending.

10 The four decisions were *Viking, Laval, Rüffert,* and *Commission v Luxembourg.* For an overview of the effects of the *Laval* Quartet on employment conditions in the countries concerned, see Seikel (2014).

(Sack 2012, p. 242). With this decision, the CJEU significantly restricted the scope of collective agreements: Collectively negotiated wages may no longer be imposed in their entirety on foreign service providers carrying out public contracts.

The *Rüffert* decision reflects a general shift in the interpretation of the freedom to provide services. While the CJEU was still applying a restrictive interpretation to the freedom to provide services well into the 1990s, since the beginning of the 2000s it has been pushing for a removal of restrictions to the freedom to provide services and an enforcement of the country of origin principle (Schmidt 2010, p. 462). As in *Laval*, the judges decided that only those provisions contained in the Posting of Workers Directive (Directive 96/71/EC) (statutory minimum wages or minimum rates of universally applicable collective agreements) could be imposed on foreign service providers. This interpretation of the directive as a maximum standard means that the directive constitutes not only a lower limit but also an upper limit for the working conditions of posted workers (Dolvik/Visser 2009, pp. 501ff.; Kempen 2010; Malmberg/Sigeman 2008, pp. 1120ff.). By doing this, the CJEU interpreted the directive as if was intended to achieve the full harmonisation of the member states' instruments for regulating wage competition through the posting of workers (Rödl 2009, p. 152), and it did so although directives, unlike regulations, basically provide for minimum conditions only.

Before the *Rüffert* decision, nine of the western German federal states had *Tariftreue* clauses. In response to *Rüffert*, some of the federal states completely abolished these clauses (Bavaria, Hesse, Schleswig-Holstein), while others restricted them to sector-related minimum wages contained in the German Act on Posted Employees (AEntG) (Hamburg, Lower Saxony). The other federal states tested how far they could go with the remaining regulatory leeway and also limited *Tariftreue* provisions to the sectors contained in the AEntG. Additionally, they introduced public-procurement-specific minimum wages and extended the list of requirements to include other such things as equal opportunity principles, core ILO (International Labour Organization) labour standards, and ecological requirements. In the meantime, fourteen German federal states have introduced new *Tariftreue* clauses, twelve including public-procurement-specific minimum wages.[11] So far only Bavaria and Saxony do not have *Tariftreue* clauses (Sack 2012, pp. 243, 253ff.; Schulten 2012; Seikel 2014).[12]

Even though it has been possible to prevent an uncontrolled lowering of labour standards, the level of social protection has definitely declined on the whole. Under

---

11   In September 2014, pursuant to a request for a preliminary ruling from Germany (C-549/13), the CJEU ruled that the public-procurement-specific minimum wage of North Rhine-Westphalia may not be demanded for services that are exclusively performed by employees employed outside of Germany. The Higher Regional Court of Koblenz also requested the CJEU in February 2014 to review the public-procurement-specific minimum wage provisions of Rhineland Palatinate (C-115/14). The Court did not object to the provision.

12   For an overview of the *Tariftreue* regulations in the various federal states, see www.boeckler.de/index_tariftreue.htm (accessed 09 August 2018).

the old *Tariftreue* regulations, contractors were obliged to apply the *entire* pay scale of the locally effective collective agreements which include wage groups for different job positions and qualifications as well as bonuses for working at night, on Sunday, and on public holidays. That was no longer permitted after the *Rüffert* decision. In areas not covered by the AEntG, posting companies could only be obliged to pay public-procurement-specific minimum wages or the statutory minimum wage implemented in 2015. But even in areas in which there were generally binding collective agreements, all that the posting companies had to comply with were the minimum-wage rates stipulated in them. The differentiated wage groups of locally effective collective agreements, however, are generally significantly higher than these. The *Rüffert* decision rendered the regulatory goals originally associated with *Tariftreue* – i.e. the stabilisation of the collective agreement system and the protection of companies and their employees bound by collective agreements from wage competition – only partially realisable.[13]

4.4 The Applicability of Collective Agreements after Transfers of Business Undertakings – The CFREU as a Vehicle of Liberalisation?[14]

Another decision that may have significant consequences for collective bargaining parties and for the scope of collective agreements is the decision of the CJEU in the *Alemo-Herron* case (C-426/11) of July 2013. In the United Kingdom, a purchaser of a privatised public company had filed a suit. In a request for a preliminary ruling from the national court, the CJEU restricted the continued applicability of collective agreements for employees after the sale of the company (technically: dynamic clauses, which are agreed to in employment contracts, that incorporate by reference the terms of collective agreements) in favour of the freedom to conduct a business/freedom to contract contained in the CFREU (Articles 15/16). The CJEU's reliance on the freedom to conduct a business and its interpretation of it is highly questionable in light of the fact that the purpose of the CFREU, at least from the point of view of trade unions and left-wing parties, is primarily the protection of the social rights of workers.[15] The CJEU used the CFREU in this case to restrict the scope of applicability of collective agreements. Furthermore, unlike in the case of single market freedoms, reliance on the CFREU means that it is not even necessary to demonstrate a cross-border element in order to use the freedom to conduct a business as an instrument for restricting those rights of workers

---

13 Shortly before *Rüffert,* Berlin and Rhineland Palatinate had been planning to extend to all sectors the *Tariftreue* clause already applied to the construction sector. This was thwarted, however, by the CJEU's decision. This illustrates that the scope of collective agreements would even have been broadened significantly without interference of the CJEU.

14 Note that the ECJ ruling in the *Asklepios* case (C-680/15, C-681/15) of 2017 which reversed the *Alemo-Herron* decision of 2013 is not taken into account in this article.

15 This was one of the reasons why the trade unions supported the Treaty of Lisbon.

which restrict the freedom of contract. This provides potential claimants with additional options for challenging market-restricting measures in the member states.

The CJEU ruled in *Alemo-Herron* that when a company is transferred to a new owner, European law forbids enforcing the purchaser to accept clauses in employment contracts that incorporate by reference collective agreements negotiated or modified after the time of the purchase (dynamic incorporation-by-reference clauses)[16] if the purchaser is unable to participate in the negotiations on the modification of the collective agreement that are made after the transfer.[17] The CJEU held that the dynamic incorporation-by-reference clauses in the case at issue would so severely restrict the purchaser's freedom of contract that his freedom to conduct a business would be unlawfully impaired; in addition, dynamic incorporation-by-reference clauses are problematic in general in light of the employer's freedom not to become a member of a business association (negative freedom of association), which the CJEU had already affirmed in its earlier decision *Werhof* (C-499/04) from 2006.

Although, in a formal sense, this decision initially only affects Great Britain, it can have consequences for other member states – including Germany – because the interpretations of EU law by the CJEU in preliminary rulings are ultimately binding for all member states. The CJEU decision could potentially impact all employees in the future who, pursuant to a transfer of business ownership, are transferred from an undertaking bound by collective agreements to one that is not, or to a purchaser that belongs to another (sectoral) business association (Lobinger 2013; Schiefer 2013). This particularly concerns privatisations in the public service sector. This decision could prove problematic for Germany in light of the far more employee-friendly attitude taken by the German Federal Labour Court in recent years in comparison to the CJEU. According to the German Federal Labour Court, incorporations of collective agreements by reference to them in employment contracts continue to apply dynamically in respect of employment contracts concluded after 31 December 2001 even if the purchaser is not bound by a collective agreement; this does not violate the freedom to choose not to associate. The decisions of the CJEU could force the German Federal Labour Court in the long run to change its position to the disadvantage of many employees. Potentially, even "static incorporations" – i.e. the general continued applicability of existing collective agreements to employees after the sale of a company – are also in danger in the medium-term.[18] In any event, the reasoning of the CJEU suggests that a regulation

---

16 "Dynamic incorporation-by-reference clauses" are clauses pursuant to which the modifications of a seller's collective agreement also apply to the employees transferred to the purchaser, even when the modifications are made after the sale.

17 The CJEU reasons that the purchaser has to be able to effectively articulate his interests and to negotiate the terms of employment of his employees in line with his future commercial activities.

18 Heuschmid (2013) does not expect major repercussions on Germany.

could already be held to infringe the freedom to conduct a business if it merely makes the purchase of a company less attractive. This may seem unrealistic at the moment, but it also shows what uncertainties exist in European law for the collective bargaining partners and for workers.

5 Conclusions

In this article, we asked what impact the jurisprudence of the CJEU has on Germany's system of industrial relations. We analysed judgments that restrict the autonomy of collective bargaining parties. As starting point served our observation that although the literature on industrial relations intensively investigates the connections between European integration and national systems of labour relations, it often ignores the influence of the CJEU.

The analysis above shows that the decisions of the CJEU have a considerable impact on Germany's collective bargaining system. The consequences are ambivalent. In decisions on anti-discrimination, the CJEU often extended the rights of employees beyond the provisions contained in national law and removed discriminating elements (on this, see for example Kokott 2010, pp. 129f.). On the downside, the judges held collective agreements that for many years had been regarded as appropriate and socially adequate to be incompatible with European law. In other areas, the CJEU took decisions that severely restrict the rights of the collective bargaining parties in a hardly justifiable way. The CJEU's jurisprudence on the fundamental freedoms has proven especially problematic. According to Rödl (2009, p. 152), in the *Rüffert* decision, the CJEU interpreted the fundamental freedoms as a legal guarantee for companies to exploit wage differences between European countries, thereby legally protecting transnational wage competition.

The CJEU often decides on specific issues in what appear to be limited individual cases. But it is only when these individual decisions are cumulated that the impact of the CJEU's decisions becomes apparent (see Werner 2013b). When the cases discussed above are looked at as a whole, it becomes clear that the right of collective bargaining and action, which is expressly guaranteed by Article 28 of the CFREU, has been restricted by the CJEU in manifold ways: It has extended the applicability of European primary and secondary law to collective agreements, it has directly censored the contents of collective agreements, it has subjected them to European procurement law, it has restricted the possibilities of regulating wage competition through collective agreements, it has virtually subordinated the right to strike to the internal market freedoms, and it has used the CFREU to restrict the applicability of collective agreements. The use of the CFREU to restrict the applicability of collective agreements after the transfer of a business undertaking is particularly bewildering in that a fundamental right was mobilised that, unlike the fundamental freedoms, does not arise from the single market rights. What can therefore be observed here is not the "radicalisation of single market integration" (Scharpf 2008, p. 19; translation: D. S./N. A.) that took place in the other cases, but a general "radicalisation" of integration through the law.

The German industrial relations model has been subjected to a process of erosion for many years now (see Ellguth/Kohaut 2017; Hassel 1999; Streeck 2009), a process that is being accelerated by the decisions of the CJEU. In addition to the legal policy changes mentioned above, the decisions of the CJEU have had two concrete effects on the freedom of collective bargaining. Firstly, they have restricted the scope, applicability, and the contents of collective agreements. Here the CJEU has reduced the group of individuals that are covered by collective agreements. This potentially affects employees of business undertakings that have been sold *(Alemo-Herron)* as well as the working conditions of posted workers (*Laval* Quartet). The result is a weakening of the protectionary function of collective agreements against wage competition and an acceleration of the erosion process in the sense that the share of the labour market covered by collective agreements is further reduced. Secondly, the decisions of the CJEU have changed the general relationship between the freedom of collective bargaining and the law. Today, the actual genuine political process of collective bargaining is being pervaded on a much larger scale by the law and by courts. In other words, the results of collective bargaining are being determined less and less by what the social partners consider correct and appropriate and more and more by what the CJEU regards as lawful. Whereas the decisions of the German Federal Labour Court for many years advocated restraint with respect to controlling contents of collective agreements[19], the CJEU's decisions have shown far less restraint in this regard.

How is this lack of restraint on the part of the CJEU, especially in the cases *Viking, Laval,* and *Rüffert,* to be explained? One explanation is the fundamental tension that exists between the single market freedoms on the one side and collective agreements and labour dispute measures on the other (Dieterich 2012, p. 97; see also Bellamy 2006; Scharpf 2009; Somek 2008). Another explanation is that the judges of the CJEU are said to have a generally pro-integrationist attitude. Analyses based on rational choice theory interpret the expansive nature of the jurisprudence as a rational strategy of the CJEU to promote its institutional interest in expanding its own powers (Höpner 2011, p. 207; this applies in general to all supranational institutions, cf. Grande 1995; Schmidt 1998, pp. 40f.; Schneider/Werle 1989). Both of these motives can, within the framework of EU treaty law, be most easily realised by passing judgments that ultimately have a liberalising effect. Thus, the political-economic consequences of integration through the law would not be consciously intended but be a side effect of a basically pro-integrationist mindset.

---

19 The so-called *Richtigkeitsgewähr* safeguards that German labour courts generally assume that collective agreements are correct. In consequence, a judicial censoring of the contents of collective agreements is prohibited.

Particularly interesting for us from a political science point of view was the interaction in the reviewed cases between legislative policy and the judge-made law of the CJEU (on this, see Schmidt 2010). Section 4.3 demonstrated how a regulation that was originally intended to have a market-correcting effect (Posted Workers Directive)[20] can, through the interaction of political and legal integration, ultimately have a liberalising effect. As discussed in section 2, governments are usually able to agree at the European level on minimum standards only, which are often below those of highly regulated countries, and/or on autonomy-preserving regulations that afford the member states leeway with respect to their implementation. The Posted Workers Directive was originally a combination of these two possibilities (on this, see Eichhorst 2000, pp. 278ff.). The idea was to prevent the circumventing of national employment standards through the enactment of minimum standards, but to still allow the member states to deviate upwards from them if they chose to (Rödl 2009, pp. 153f.). However, the *Laval* Quartet shows that in cases in which the minimum standards in a European directive that was originally intended as *market-correcting* measure are below the standards of a member state, the CJEU's interpretation can ultimately lead to a *decline* in social standards.

Equally interesting from a political science point of view is what happened in response to the attempt to correct politically the *Laval* decision. In reaction to the decisions of the *Laval* Quartet, trade unions and the European Parliament put pressure on the European Commission to start an initiative to correct the CJEU decisions. The result of this was the draft legislation known as the Monti-II Regulation, which the Commission presented in 2012.[21] The intention of the trade unions was to rebalance the relation between the right to take collective actions and the freedom of establishment and the freedom to provide services at the level of secondary law. But the Commission's draft of the regulation merely codified the existing case law of the CJEU. Furthermore, it contained provisions on a dispute resolution mechanism and imposed reporting ob-

---

20 At least from the point of view of the countries receiving posted workers (Belgium, Denmark, Germany, France, the Netherlands) Directive 96/71/EC was meant to have a market-correcting function. It is unclear, however, the extent to which the Commission and the posting countries (Greece, Ireland, Italy, Portugal, Spain) had the same intention. As mentioned by Eichhorst (1999; 2000) and Sörries (1997), an agreement on the directive became possible after some countries had gone ahead on their own and introduced their own regulations for posted workers. One reason why the posting countries and the Commission granted their consent was because the directive provided at least a minimum of influence over the national regulations of the countries that had barged ahead on their own. Directive 96/71/EC is ultimately a crossbreed of market restriction and an attempt to prevent an uncoordinated introduction of even more, allegedly protectionist, regulations (on this ambivalence from a legal perspective, see Davies 1997).

21 The Enforcement Directive (Directive 2004/48/EC) also belonged to the so-called Monti-II package. This was, however, something that had been demanded for a long time already, and was not aimed at correcting the *Laval* decision.

ligations for strikes in cases where the functioning of the single market could be impaired by labour disputes. This would have implied an even more far-reaching restriction of the collective rights of trade unions (Schubert 2012). After a sufficiently large number of national parliaments filed a subsidiarity complaint – the first in the history of the EU – the Commission withdrew the proposal. A coalition composed of the European Parliament and the trade unions has been unsuccessful to date in turning these decisions around. This clearly illustrates just how little latitude there is for politically correcting the decisions of the Court of Justice in the current circumstances (Commission's monopolised right of legislative initiative, influence of the Directorate-General on the internal market, opposing interests of the member states).[22]

What consequences do these findings have for highly coordinated economies such as Germany, i.e. systems in which the social partners have a large degree of regulatory autonomy? In corporatist models like the German model, collective negotiations and industrial actions are central mechanisms for regulating the economy. These mechanisms have been weakened by the decisions of the CJEU. The emphasising of the single market freedoms also shifts the power relationship between capital and labour to the disadvantage of trade unions (see Scharpf 2010b, pp. 221f.). It disrupts the specific balance between social regulation and economic freedom of the organised capitalism model (see Höpner 2008, p.18). As to whether the decisions of the CJEU discussed in this article, particularly the decisions in *Viking, Laval,* and *Rüffert,* are causing a transformation of industrial relations in Germany towards a market-liberal model is something that cannot be conclusively answered on the basis of the cases reviewed here. Such an assessment would necessitate a systematic review of the effects that integration through law has on other areas, such as the CJEU's jurisprudence in the area of corporate governance and its impact on co-determination.[23]

How can the jurisprudence of the CJEU, which seems to have got out of control, be curbed? A variety of possibilities are being considered in the public and academic debate. The European Trade Union Confederation is calling for a Social Progress Protocol to be added to the EU Treaties with the intention of establishing the priority of fundamental social rights over the fundamental freedoms. Some scholars suggest injecting an "antidote" into secondary law, for example by generalising the logic of the *Albany* decision in a form of an EU regulation (Heuschmid 2018; Höpner 2017; Kingreen 2014). Another proposal involves the establishment of a competence-monitoring court as a counterweight to the CJEU (see Roman Herzog and Lüder Gerken in the Frankfurter Allgemeine Zeitung of 8 September 2008). Finally, another suggestion is to set up specialised chambers within the CJEU, the assumption being that specialised chambers for

---

22 See footnote 9 regarding the recent revision of the Posted Workers Directive.

23 For example *Commission v Germany* (C-112/05, see Werner 2013a), *Erzberger* (C-566/15) and *Polbud* (C-106/16).

labour law would treat collective bargaining systems of the member states more care-fully and would be better able to understand the idiosyncrasies of national labour laws.

REFERENCES

Alter, K. (2001): Establishing the supremacy of European law. The making of an international rule of law in Europe, Oxford

Behrens, M. (2013): Germany, in: Frege, C. / Kelly, J. (eds.): Comparative employment relations in the global economy, London, pp. 206–226

Bellamy, R. (2006): Still in deficit: Rights, regulation, and democracy in the EU, in: European Law Journal 12 (6), pp. 725–742

Busch, K. / Hermann, C. / Hinrichs, K. / Schulten, T. (2013): Euro crisis, austerity policy and the European social model. How crisis policies in southern Europe threaten the EU's social dimension, Berlin

Davies, P. (1997): Posted workers: single market or protection of national labour law systems?, in: Common Market Law Review 34 (3), pp. 571–602

Dieterich, T. (2012): Europäische Grundrechts-Rechtsprechung – Kooperation und Kollisionen, in: Creutzfeldt, M. / Hanau, P. / Thüsing, G. / Wißmann, H. (eds.): Arbeitsgerichtsbarkeit und Wissen-schaft. Festschrift für Klaus Bepler zum 65. Geburtstag, Munich, pp. 87–100

Dolvik, J. E. / Visser, J. (2009): Free movement, equal treatment and workers' rights: can the European Union solve its trilemma of fundamental principles?, in: Industrial Relations Journal 40 (6), pp. 491–509

Eichhorst, W. (1999): Europäische marktgestaltende Politik zwischen Supranationalität und nationa-ler Autonomie: Das Beispiel der Entsenderichtline, in: Industrielle Beziehungen 6 (3), pp. 340–359

Eichhorst, W. (2000): Europäische Sozialpolitik zwischen nationaler Autonomie und Marktfreiheit. Die Entsendung von Arbeitnehmern in der EU, Frankfurt a. M.

Ellguth, P. / Kohaut, S. (2017): Tarifbindung und betriebliche Interessenvertretung: Ergebnisse aus dem IAB-Betriebspanel 2016, in: WSI-Mitteilungen 70 (4), pp. 278–286

Falkner, G. / Treib, O. / Hartlapp, M. / Leiber, S. (2005): Complying with Europe. EU harmonisation and soft law in the member states, Cambridge

Fischer-Lescano, A. (2014): Austeritätspolitik und Menschenrechte. Rechtspflichten der Unionsor-gane beim Abschluss von Memoranda of Understanding. Rechtsgutachten im Auftrag der Kammer für Arbeiter/innen und Angestellte für Wien

Grahl, J. / Teague, P. (2005): Problems of financial integration in the EU, in: Journal of European Public Policy 12 (6), pp. 1005–1021

Grande, E. (1995): Forschungspolitik in der Politikverflechtungs-Falle? Institutionelle Strukturen, Konfliktdimensionen und Verhandlungslogiken europäischer Forschungs- und Technologiepolitik, in: Politische Vierteljahresschrift 36 (3), pp. 460–483

Hassel, A. (1999): The erosion of the German system of industrial relations, in: British Journal of Industrial Relations 37 (3), pp. 483–505

Heuschmid, J. (2013): Dynamische Bezugnahmeklauseln beim Betriebsübergang, in: Arbeit und Recht 61 (12), pp. 498–502

Heuschmid, J. (2018): Der Arbeitskampf im EU-Recht, in: Däubler, W. (ed.): Arbeitskampfrecht. Handbuch für die Rechtspraxis, Baden-Baden, pp. 162–232

Höpner, M. (2008): Usurpation statt Delegation. Wie der EuGH die Binnenmarktintegration radikali-siert und warum er politischer Kontrolle bedarf, Köln

Höpner, M. (2011): Der Europäische Gerichtshof als Motor der Integration: Eine akteursbezogene Erklärung, in: Berliner Journal für Soziologie 21 (2), pp. 203–229

Höpner, M. (2013): Soziale Demokratie? Die polit-ökonomische Heterogenität Europas als Determinante des demokratischen und sozialen Potenzials der Europäischen Union, in: Europarecht Beiheft 1/2013, pp. 69–89

Höpner, M. (2017): The Social Progress Protocol of the ETUC. A suggestion for its future development, Düsseldorf

Höpner, M. / Schäfer, A. (2010): A new phase of European integration, in: West European Politics 33 (2), pp. 344–368

Hyman, R. (2001): The Europeanisation – or the erosion – of industrial relation?, in: Industrial Relations Journal 32 (4), pp. 280–294

Kempen, O. E. (2010): Das Grundrecht der Koalitionsfreiheit vor dem Europäischen Gerichtshof, in: Dieterich, T. / Le Friant, M. / Nogler, L. / Kezuka, K. / Pfarr, H. (eds.): Individuelle und kollektive Freiheit im Arbeitsrecht. Gedächtnisschrift für Ulrich Zachert, Baden-Baden, pp. 15–36

Keune, M. (2008): Die Grenzen der europäischen Arbeitsmarktintegration: Koalitionen, Interessenvielfalt und institutionelle Hindernisse, in: Höpner, M. / Schäfer, A. (eds.): Die Politische Ökonomie der europäischen Integration, Frankfurt a. M., pp. 279–309

Kingreen, T. (2014): Soziale Fortschrittsklausel – Potenzial und Alternativen, Frankfurt a. M.

Kocher, E. (2009): Stoppt den EuGH? Zum Ort der Politik einer europäischen Arbeitsverfassung, in: Fischer-Lescano, A. / Rödl, F. / Schmid, C. U. (eds.): Europäische Gesellschaftsverfassung. Zur Konstitutionalisierung sozialer Demokratie in Europa, Baden-Baden, pp. 161–179

Kocher, E. (2010): Europäische Tarifautonomie – Rechtsrahmen für Autonomie und Korporatismus, in: juridikum 4/2010, pp. 465–483

Kokott, J. (2010): Der EuGH – eine neoliberale Institution?, in: Hohmann-Dennhardt, C. / Masuch, P. / Villiger, M. (eds.): Grundrechte und Solidarität. Durchsetzung und Verfahren, Kehl, pp. 115–134

Lillie, N. / Greer, I. (2007): Industrial relations, migration, and neoliberal politics: The case of the European construction sector, in: Politics & Society 35 (4), pp. 551–581

Lobinger, T. (2013): EuGH zur dynamischen Bezugnahme von Tarifverträgen bei Betriebsübergängen, in: Neue Zeitschrift für Arbeitsrecht 17/2013, pp. 945–947

Malmberg, J. / Sigeman, T. (2008): Industrial actions and EU economic freedoms, in: Common Market Law Journal 45 (4), pp. 1115–1146

Marginson, P. (2006): Europeanisation and regime competition: industrial relations and EU enlargement, in: Industrielle Beziehungen 13 (2), pp. 97–117

Marginson, P. / Sisson, K. (2006): European integration and industrial relations. Multi-level governance in the making, Houndmills

Rhodes, M. (1998): Globalisation, labour markets and welfare states: a future of "competitive corporatism"?, in: Rhodes, M. / Mény, Y. (eds.): The future of European welfare, Basingstoke

Rödl, F. (2009): Transnationale Lohnkonkurrenz: ein neuer Eckpfeiler der „sozialen" Union?, in: Fischer-Lescano, A. / Rödl, F. / Schmid, C. U. (eds.): Europäische Gesellschaftsverfassung. Zur Konstitutionalisierung sozialer Demokratie in Europa, Baden-Baden, pp. 145–160

Sack, D. (2012): Europeanization through law, compliance, and party differences. The ECJ's 'Rüffert' judgment (C-346/06) and amendments to public procurement laws in German federal states, in: Journal of European Integration 34 (3), pp. 241–260

Schäfer, A. / Streeck, W. (2008): Korporatismus in der Europäischen Union, in: Höpner, M. / Schäfer, A. (eds.): Die Politische Ökonomie der europäischen Integration, Frankfurt a. M., pp. 203–240

Scharpf, F. W. (2008): „Der einzige Weg ist, dem EuGH nicht zu folgen", in: Mitbestimmung 07+08/2008, pp. 18–23

Scharpf, F. W. (2009): Legitimacy in the multilevel European polity, in: European Political Science Review 1 (2), pp. 173–204

Scharpf, F. W. (2010a): Negative and positive integration in the political economy of European welfare states, in: Scharpf, F. W. (ed.): Community and autonomy. Institutions, policies and legitimacy in multilevel Europe, Frankfurt a. M., pp. 91–126

Scharpf, F. W. (2010b): The asymmetry of European integration, or why the EU cannot be a "social market economy", in: Socio-Economic Review 8 (2), pp. 211–250

Schiefer, B. (2013): Ende der Dynamik einer arbeitsvertraglichen Bezugnahme im Falle eines Betriebsübergangs, in: Betriebs-Berater 43/2013, pp. 2613–2615

Schmidt, S. K. (1998): Liberalisierung in Europa. Die Rolle der Europäischen Kommission, Frankfurt a. M.

Schmidt, S. K. (2010): Gefangen im "lock-in"?, in: Der moderne Staat 3 (2), pp. 455–473

Schneider, V. / Werle, R. (1989): Vom Regime zum korporativen Akteur. Zur institutionellen Dynamik der Europäischen Gemeinschaft, in: Kohler-Koch, B. (ed.): Regime in den internationalen Beziehungen, Baden-Baden, pp. 409–434

Schubert, J. (2012): Der Vorschlag der EU-Kommission für eine Monti-II-Verordnung. Eine kritische Analyse unter Einbeziehung der Überlegungen zur Enforcement-Richtlinie, Saarbrücken

Schulten, T. (2012): Germany, in: Schulten, T. / Alsos, K. / Burgess, P. / Pedersen, K. (eds.): Pay and other social clauses in European public procurement. An overview on regulation and practices with a focus on Denmark, Germany, Norway, Switzerland and the United Kingdom, Düsseldorf, pp. 53–71

Schulten, T. / Müller, T. (2013): Ein neuer europäischer Interventionismus?, in: Wirtschaft und Gesellschaft 39 (3), pp. 291–321

Seikel, D. (2014): How the European Commission deepened financial market integration. The battle over the liberalization of public banks in Germany, in: Journal of European Public Policy 21 (2), pp. 169–187

Seikel, D. (2018): Entsendung: Politik muss neue Möglichkeiten zur Begrenzung von Lohnwettbewerb nutzen, Work on Progress, https://www.boeckler.de/wsi_blog_114125.htm (accessed 16 January 2019)

Somek, A. (2008): Individualism: An essay on the authority of the European Union, Oxford

Sörries, B. (1997): Die Entsenderichtlinie: Entscheidungsprozess und Rückkoppelungen im Mehrebenensystem, in: Industrielle Beziehungen 4 (2), pp. 125–149

Streeck, W. (1998): The internationalization of industrial relations in Europe: Prospects and problems, in: Politics & Society 26 (4), pp. 429–459

Streeck, W. (2000): Competitive solidarity: Rethinking the "European Social Model", in: Hinrichs, K. / Kitschelt, H. / Wiesenthal, H. (eds.): Kontingenz und Krise. Institutionenpolitik in kapitalistischen und postsozialistischen Gesellschaften, Frankfurt a. M., pp. 245–261

Streeck, W. (2009): Re-forming capitalism. Institutional change in the German political economy, Oxford

Teague, P. (1999): Economic citizenship in the European Union. Employment relations in the new Europe, London

Visser, J. (2005): Beneath the surface of stability. New and old modes of governance in European industrial relations, in: European Journal of Industrial Relations 11 (3), pp. 287–306

Vos, K. J. (2006): Europeanization and convergence in industrial relations, in: European Journal of Industrial Relations 12 (3), pp. 311–327

Weiler, J. H. H. (1994): A quiet revolution. The European Court of Justice and its interlocutors, in: Comparative Political Studies 26 (4), pp. 510–534

Werner, B. (2013a): Der Streit um das VW-Gesetz. Wie Europäische Kommission und Europäischer Gerichtshof die Unternehmenskontrolle liberalisieren, Frankfurt a. M.

Werner, B. (2013b): Ein zahnloser Tiger?, in: Leviathan 41 (3), pp. 358–382

Woolfson, C. / Thörnqvist, C. / Sommers, J. (2010): The Swedish model and the future of labour standards after Laval, in: Industrial Relations Journal 41 (4), pp. 333–350

Zeibig, N. (2013a): Altersdiskriminierung in der Arbeitswelt – Gerichtliche Entscheidungen im Überblick, in: WSI-Mitteilungen 66 (5), pp. 369–372

Zeibig, N. (2013b): Questions of age discrimination in decisions of the European Court of Justice, in: Grozelier, A.-M. / Hacker, B. / Kowalsky, W. / Machnig, J. / Meyer, H. / Unger, B. (eds.): Roadmap to a social Europe, pp. 126–128

AUTHORS

DANIEL SEIKEL, Dr., is head of the research unit European Policies at the Institute of Economic and Social Research (WSI) of the Hans-Böckler-Foundation.

@ E-Mail: daniel-seikel@boeckler.de

NADINE ABSENGER, Dr., is head of the law department of the German trade union confederation DGB.

@ E-Mail: Nadine.Absenger@dgb.de

Abstracts · Zusammenfassungen

THORSTEN SCHULTEN

German Collective Bargaining – from Erosion to Revitalisation?

For more than two decades Germany has seen a continuous decline in collective bargaining coverage leading to a significant erosion of the overall bargaining systems. In the meantime, all relevant social actors have expressed the view that new initiatives are necessary to reverse that trend. The article is basically composed of two parts; the first part contains a detailed analysis of the development of collective bargaining in Germany and elaborates the available data on collective bargaining coverage. In the second part, the current fundamental approaches and concrete proposals for a revitalisation of German collective bargaining from trade unions, employers' associations and political actors are discussed.

Tarifverhandlungen in Deutschland – von der Erosion zur Revitalisierung?

Seit mehr als zwei Jahrzehnten geht die Tarifbindung in Deutschland kontinuierlich zurück und hat bereits zu einer erheblichen Erosion des gesamten Tarifvertragssystems geführt. Mittlerweile haben alle relevanten sozialen Akteure ihre Überzeugung zum Ausdruck gebracht, dass neue Initiativen nötig sind, um diesen Trend wieder umzukehren. Der Beitrag besteht im Wesentlichen aus zwei Teilen. Der erste Teil enthält eine detaillierte Analyse über die Entwicklung der Tarifverhandlungen in Deutschland und untersucht die aktuell verfügbaren Daten zur Tarifbindung. Im zweiten Teil diskutiert der Autor grundlegende Ansätze und konkrete Vorschläge für eine Revitalisierung der Tarifpolitik, wie sie aktuell von Gewerkschaften, Arbeitgeberverbänden und politischen Akteuren in die Debatte eingebracht werden.

MARTIN BEHRENS, HEINER DRIBBUSCH

Avoiding the Union at the Workplace
Evidence from Surveys amongst German Trade Unions

This article presents the findings of a 2015 survey amongst local trade union organisations on employer resistance to works councils. It is a follow-up study to a similar survey conducted by the WSI in 2012. The evidence confirms that the first establishment of a works council is a contested issue. The obstruction of the election of works councils by employers is found in particular amongst owner-operated small and medium-sized establishments. The article initially puts employer resistance to works councils in the context of the German system of industrial relations and presents the survey and its evidence. It concludes with a brief discussion of the extent to which the frequency of employer resistance to works councils is reported by union officials and how this reporting is influenced by the structure of the local industry and union activity.

Wie Gewerkschaften aus den Betrieben ferngehalten werden
Befunde aus Umfragen unter deutschen Gewerkschaften

Dieser Beitrag präsentiert die Ergebnisse einer 2015 bei lokalen Gewerkschaftsorganisationen durchgeführten Untersuchung zum Widerstand von Arbeitgebern gegen Betriebsräte. Es handelt sich um eine Folgestudie zu einer ähnlichen Umfrage des WSI aus dem Jahr 2012. Die Befunde bestätigen, dass bereits die Gründung eines Betriebsrats ein umstrittenes Thema ist. Die Behinderung der Wahl von Betriebsräten durch Arbeitgeber findet sich insbesondere bei inhabergeführten kleinen und mittleren Betrieben. Der Beitrag stellt den Arbeitgeber-Widerstand zunächst in den Kontext des deutschen Systems der Arbeitsbeziehungen und stellt sodann die Erhebung und ihre Resultate vor. Abschließend wird kurz diskutiert, in welchem Umfang arbeitgeberseitiger Widerstand gegen Betriebsräte von Gewerkschaftsfunktionären berichtet wird und wie diese Berichterstattung durch die Struktur der lokalen Industrie und die Gewerkschaftsaktivitäten beeinflusst wird.

HELGE EMMLER, WOLFRAM BREHMER

The Composition of German Works Councils
Results from the WSI Works Council Survey

The article describes the personnel composition of works councils using the representative WSI Works Council Surveys 2015 and 2018. In addition to socio-demographic characteristics this survey allows investigation of full-time works councils, their terms of office, their forms of employment and union density. The second step of this article involves comparing the characteristics of the members of the works councils with the personnel composition of the respective workforces. This comparison enables the authors to demonstrate which groups are under- or overrepresented in the works councils. The findings suggest that whereas the level of educational attainment of works council members corresponds largely to that of the workforce, other characteristics are underrepresented; women are less likely to be works council members than men. Employees with migrant backgrounds represent about 17 % of the workforces, but only 8.5 % of the works councils. Temporary workers are underrepresented; the proportion of temporary workers on works councils represents only a tenth of the numbers of those employed.

Die Zusammensetzung von Betriebsräten in Deutschland
Ergebnisse der WSI-Betriebsrätebefragungen

Dieser Beitrag beschreibt die Zusammensetzung deutscher Betriebsräte mit repräsentativen Daten der WSI-Betriebsrätebefragungen 2015 und 2018. Neben soziodemografischen Merkmalen werden dabei auch Freistellungen, Amtszeiten, Organisationsgrade und Beschäftigungsformen berücksichtigt. In einem zweiten Schritt werden die Merkmale der Betriebsräte den Merkmalen der Belegschaften in den jeweiligen Betrieben gegenübergestellt. So kann aufgezeigt werden, welche Beschäftigtengruppen in welchem Maße (dis-)proportional im Betriebsrat vertreten sind. Während Betriebsräte in Bezug auf ihre Bildungsabschlüsse weitgehend den Belegschaften zu entsprechen scheinen, sind andere Merkmale in den Betriebsräten zum Teil deutlich unterrepräsentiert; Frauen sind um etwa fünf Prozentpunkte seltener im Betriebsrat als in der Belegschaft vertreten, Beschäftigte mit Migrationshintergrund finden sich doppelt so häufig in der Belegschaft wie im Betriebsrat, und befristet Beschäftigte haben in Betriebsräten sogar nur ein Zehntel des Anteils inne, den sie in den Belegschaften ausmachen.

ANKE HASSEL, WOLFGANG SCHROEDER

Trade Union Membership Policy: the Key to Stronger Social Partnership

German trade unions have suffered for a number of decades from declining membership, representation gaps and problems enforcing strong collective bargaining. The article analyses the pattern of union membership in international comparison and discusses new approaches towards trade union membership policies. It thereby focuses on systematic approaches of organising strategies in the metal sector and the increasing use of membership surveys in order to establish members' preferences and strengthen the legitimacy of trade union strategies in collective bargaining.

Gewerkschaftliche Mitgliederpolitik:
Schlüssel für eine starke Sozialpartnerschaft

Die deutschen Gewerkschaften leiden seit mehreren Jahrzehnten an rückläufigen Mitgliederzahlen, Vertretungslücken in der Mitgliederstruktur und einer Durchsetzungskrise in der Tarifpolitik. Der Beitrag analysiert die Mitgliederentwicklung der DGB-Gewerkschaften im internationalen Vergleich und die Möglichkeiten von neuen Ansätzen der Mitgliederpolitik. Dabei wird insbesondere die systematische Erschließung neuer Mitglieder in der IG Metall betrachtet wie auch die zunehmende Nutzung von Mitglieder- und Beschäftigtenbefragungen als Instrument der Erfassung von Mitgliederpräferenzen, um die Legitimation gewerkschaftlichen Handelns in der Tarifpolitik zu stärken.

HEINER DRIBBUSCH

New Militancy in a Changing Industrial Landscape
The Migration of Industrial Action to the German Service Sector

The article focuses on the shift of industrial action from (metal) manufacturing to the service sector which has been observed in Germany since the mid-2000s. This "tertiarisation of conflict" took place against the background of structural changes in the service sector following liberalisation and deregulation of public services. The article gives an overview of the quantitative and qualitative aspects of the increase of industrial action in the service sector. It shows that new groups of workers such as medical doctors, nurses, child care workers, train drivers or security staff who did not have a record of strike activity in the past have now shaped the picture of industrial conflict in Germany. Focusing on the United Services Union, ver.di, the article sheds a light on forms, outcomes and challenges of strikes in private and public services.

Neue Militanz in einer sich wandelnden Wirtschaftslandschaft
Die Verlagerung des deutschen Arbeitskampfgeschehens in den Dienstleistungssektor

Der Artikel befasst sich mit der Verschiebung des Arbeitskampfgeschehens von der (Metall-) Industrie hin zum Dienstleistungssektor. Diese sogenannte „Tertiarisierung" des Arbeitskampfs fand vor dem Hintergrund struktureller Veränderungen im Dienstleistungsbereich statt, die maßgeblich durch die Liberalisierung und Deregulierung des öffentlichen Sektors ausgelöst wurden. Der Artikel gibt einen Überblick über die quantitativen und qualitativen Aspekte des Anstiegs von Arbeitskämpfen in den Dienstleistungsbranchen. Er zeigt, dass neue Beschäftigtengruppen wie z. B. Ärzte und Ärztinnen, Krankenpfleger*innen, Erzieher*innen, Lokführer*innen oder Sicherheitsleute, die früher nicht für Streiks bekannt waren, inzwischen das Arbeitskampfgeschehen prägen. Mit speziellem Blick auf ver.di werden Formen, Ergebnisse sowie Herausforderungen von Streiks im Dienstleistungssektor beleuchtet.

DANIEL SEIKEL, NADINE ABSENGER

The Impact of the Jurisprudence of the Court of Justice of the European Union on Germany's Collective Bargaining System

The rulings of the Court of Justice of the European Union (CJEU) in the cases of Laval (C-341/05), Viking (C-438/05), Rüffert (C-346/06) and Commission v Luxembourg (C-319/06) have demonstrated that the Court's adjudication has substantial effects on national systems of industrial relations. This article examines the consequences of the case law of the CJEU on the collective bargaining system in Germany from a law and political science perspective. The authors examine selected CJEU rulings and show that the Court's adjudication restricts the rights and room for manoeuvre of social partners, affecting the right to strike as well as specific regulations in collective agreements. In the area of individual labour law, the CJEU regularly rules in favour of employees. However, when it comes to collective labour law, the Court often decides to the detriment of collective bargaining autonomy. This weakens collective social rights.

Die Auswirkungen der EuGH-Rechtsprechung
auf das Tarifvertragssystem in Deutschland

Spätestens seit den Urteilen des Europäischen Gerichtshofs (EuGH) in den Fällen Laval (C-341/05), Viking (C-438/05), Rüffert (C-346/06) und Kommission gegen Luxemburg (C-319/06) ist deutlich geworden, dass die Rechtsprechung des Gerichtshofs erhebliche Auswirkungen auf die nationalen Systeme industrieller Beziehungen hat. Dieser Artikel untersucht aus politik- und rechtswissenschaftlicher Perspektive, welche Folgen die EuGH-Rechtsprechung auf das Tarifvertragssystem in Deutschland hat. Anhand von ausgewählten EuGH-Entscheidungen zeigen die Autoren, dass die Rechtsprechung des Gerichtshofes häufig Rechte und Handlungsmöglichkeiten von Tarifparteien einschränkt, angefangen beim Streikrecht bis hin zur Ausgestaltung und Geltung von Tarifverträgen. Während der EuGH im Bereich des individuellen Arbeitsrechts oft zugunsten der Arbeitnehmerinteressen entscheidet, gehen Urteile zum kollektiven Arbeitsrecht häufig zu Lasten der Tarifautonomie. Kollektive Selbstbestimmungsrechte werden dadurch geschwächt.